PUTTING

IT

ALL

TOGETHER

*Exploring the Basic Tenets
of Christian Discipleship*

William Roger Matkin, D. Min.

ISBN: 9798364502858

This edition is published by William Roger Matkin of Boerne, Texas
Printed in the United States of America

OTHER BOOKS
BY
WILLIAM ROGER MATKIN

Keeping Your Eyes Open
Seeing God's Hand in the Ordinary

Lessons From Doctor Luke
Bible Studies For Individuals and Small Groups

TABLE OF CONTENTS

PRACTICAL TOOLS AND RELATED MATERIALS

PREFACE

To appreciate this book, it will be helpful for you to understand the author, where he is coming from, his background, etc. Beginning in college at Texas A&M, I studied Electrical Engineering, Mathematics, and Physics, and after four years, graduated with a BA degree in Mathematics and Physics. That's important because it tells you that I'm the kind of person who needs to know how things work, how they fit together, and how they are organized. If it doesn't *make sense* to me, I cannot pass it on to others. And so it was as I began my career as a Campus Minister after graduation from seminary. You may be wondering about the road I traveled getting from Texas A&M to the seminary. The long and short of it is that during my last couple of years of college, I felt a clear and certain call to the ministry.

My primary role was discipler and enabler with undergraduate and graduate students to move them along the path of spiritual growth and becoming disciples of Jesus Christ. From the beginning, I made every effort to have a grasp of the *big picture* of the Christian faith and what it means to become a serious follower of Jesus Christ. My seminary training was very helpful in that regard and gave me a brand new perspective, especially historically speaking, as my undergraduate curriculum was devoid of that arena. Over the 41 years of my campus ministry career, my ideas were refined, organized, and I eventually designed a course I offered to students each semester called *Discipleship 101*. The course was built around the diagram you'll find on page 11. The title, *Discipleship Model*, says it all. It may not be the whole story about what it means to be a serious follower of Jesus Christ, but it represents what makes sense to me based on my life-long study of God's Word and my real-life experience with college and graduate students over my career.

I hope that the words and ideas expressed in this book will make sense to you and help you get a grasp for yourself of the basic tenets of the Christian walk ... in essence, *putting it all together* for you.

Roger Matkin, 2023

ACKNOWLEDGEMENTS

Over my forty-one years in campus ministry, I served in three Texas cities: Weatherford, Fort Worth, and San Antonio, and with two highly respected organizations, Baptist Student Union (BSU, now named Baptist Student Ministries), and Christian Medical & Dental Association (CMDA).

For the first 25 years, I worked for BSU and served under three state BSU Directors: Dr. W.F. Howard, Chet Reames, and Jack Greever. I am grateful to have learned my craft well under the direction and guidance of these three gifted men. I am also grateful for my colleagues, and fellow BSU Directors, with whom I worked during those years. Putting It All Together is intensely practical and it was in the day-to-day doing of my ministry with students that I developed the ideas and strategies that permeate this book.

During the final sixteen years of my ministry, I had the privilege of plying my craft in a *new* arena, CMDA. I am grateful to the leadership of CMDA for giving me that opportunity, in particular, to David Stevens, MD, CEO, and Gene Rudd, MD, Senior Vice President. I was given the freedom to develop a ministry in San Antonio to students and professionals that would become the CMDA model for the USA. Our first San Antonio CMDA Council President, Wayne Grant, MD, is representative of the quality of men and women who have given themselves sacrificially to the Lord and the ministry over the last three decades, which made CMDA SA what it is today. I am indebted to Autumn Dawn Galbreath, MD. Former student and friend, for her attention to detail in reading and editing the manuscript. Putting It All Together is a better book thanks to her efforts.

The content of Putting It All Together is mine and was developed over many years on the anvil of experience. However, for this book, I would be remiss if I did not acknowledge the one person responsible for the great majority of the editing, final layout, graphic arts, etc. That person is my wife and life partner of 55 years, Melva. It was she who came up with the book's cover, i.e., puzzle pieces, which is the perfect metaphor to introduce this book. Her skill with a computer is nothing short of amazing as she is self-taught. She has spent countless hours working on my behalf, and I will be eternally grateful for her sacrificial service and expertise. No Melva, no Putting It All Together ever being published.

INTRODUCTION

The Creeds of the ancient church were attempts at *putting it all together* doctrinally and theologically speaking. There were schisms within the body of believers resulting in disorder and divisions. Heresies were prevalent and out there for public consumption - both in danger of marginalizing Christianity to the general population. Creeds are extremely important documents and are used even today in the modern church to schematize and standardize our understanding of God.

The Nicene Creed, carefully crafted with a penchant for detail, was formalized at the Council of Nicea in 325 AD. The stated purpose was to provide a statement of correct belief or orthodoxy: it was drawn up in times of doctrinal conflict. Classic creeds clarified and codified the key concepts of the Christian faith.

> *We believe in one God, the Father, the Almighty, maker of heaven and earth, Of all that is, seen and unseen.*
> *We believe in one Lord, Jesus Christ, the only Son of God, eternally begotten of the Father, God from God, Light from Light, true God from true God, begotten, not made, of one Being with the Father. Through him, all things were made. For us and our salvation, he came down from heaven: by the power of the Holy Spirit, he became incarnate from the Virgin Mary and was made man.*
> *For our sake he was crucified under Pontius Pilate; he suffered death and was buried.*
> *On the third day, he rose again in accordance with the Scriptures; he ascended into heaven and is seated at the right hand of the Father.*
> *He will come again in glory to judge the living and the dead, and his kingdom will have no end.*
> *We believe in the Holy Spirit, the Lord, the giver of life who proceeds from the Father and the Son. With the Father and the Son, he is worshipped and glorified. He has spoken through the Prophets.*
> *We believe in one holy catholic and apostolic Church.*
> *We acknowledge one baptism for the forgiveness of sins.*
> *We look for the resurrection of the dead and the life of the world to come. Amen*

The Apostles Creed, more compact, was another early statement of Christian belief used in church liturgies and teaching. It was first mentioned in 390 AD and named because of the assumption that the Twelve Apostles contributed to the core of the Creed.

> I believe in God, the Father almighty, creator of heaven and earth.
> I believe in Jesus Christ, his only Son, our Lord,
> who was conceived by the Holy Spirit, born of the Virgin Mary,
> suffered under Pontius Pilate, was crucified died, and was buried;
> he descended to the dead.
> On the third day, he rose again; he ascended into heaven,
> He is seated at the right hand of the Father,
> And he will come to judge the living and the dead.
> I believe in the Holy Spirit,
> The holy catholic church,
> The communion of the saints, the forgiveness of sins,
> The resurrection of the body, and the life everlasting. Amen

Putting It All Together (PIAT) is the author's attempt to organize and formalize accepted beliefs about Christian theology, doctrine, and practice - the actual day-to-day implementation of what one believes. Until doctrine gets to the *street level*, it is not of much value to the ongoing worldwide Kingdom of God. This book represents the practical application of the author's belief system, i.e., what I understand regarding what Jesus said to his original disciples as to how they were to live out their lives for Him and His Kingdom.

As these two creeds illustrate, there is no one way of expressing the basic truths of Christianity. They are similar, yet different. There is no one true creed. Neither is there one true way of doing Christianity, practically speaking. **PIAT** makes no such claim. But it does represent what God has revealed to this author and the conclusions reached over a lifetime on the anvil of experience.

The **Model of Biblical Discipleship** is the summation and graphic expression of those conclusions. It is intended to be interpreted from the center to the periphery. The overarching idea is integration, i.e. how the concepts dovetail with each other. The center circle is the most significant, powerful, and critical component – our relationship with our Creator, Father, and Redeemer.

Before we get into the particulars of the Model, it is important to understand the mindset that will be required to implement the ideas being suggested in this book in daily living. That mindset can be generally described as *intentionality*. Entropy is defined as a measure of the degree of disorder in a system undergoing change. Entropy always increases over time, i.e., systems tend to self-destruct, degrade, get worse, become less organized, and have less energy over time. For example, orbiting satellites, without correction, tend to deteriorate and will eventually fall into the earth's atmosphere and burn up. More examples: gardens and lawns get weeds, people age, their bodies are in perpetual decay, and without effort to the contrary, they become overweight and out of shape.

The good news is that the Law of Entropy, even though it cannot be defeated, can be held at bay with *intentional effort* on the part of us humans. Well-tended gardens produce abundant fruit and vegetables; beautifully, manicured vineyards cover the hills in California's Napa Valley; satellites can maintain stable trajectories with timely human intervention; with effort and intentionality, folks can stay reasonably healthy and fit throughout their lives.

All of these metaphors transfer quite handily to the spiritual realm. So if a person wants to remain or become a healthy, happy, fruitful disciple of Jesus Christ, it will happen in the same manner – with intentionality, and deliberate effort. There are no shortcuts, the Law of Entropy applies here as well. Introducing the reader to that process is what PIAT is about.

Question: If nothing changes in your life spiritually speaking, if life goes on as it has been going on, and if you stay on the same track, then can you expect any substantial change in your life as a disciple of Jesus? But to the contrary, if as a result of implementing some of the ideas presented here, you begin to incorporate some new habits, disciplines, tools, and new ways of thinking and living, then eventually your new lifestyle will begin to have a significant impact on your relationship to the living God and his Son, Jesus.

4

DISCIPLESHIP MODEL

By William Roger Matkin, D.Min.

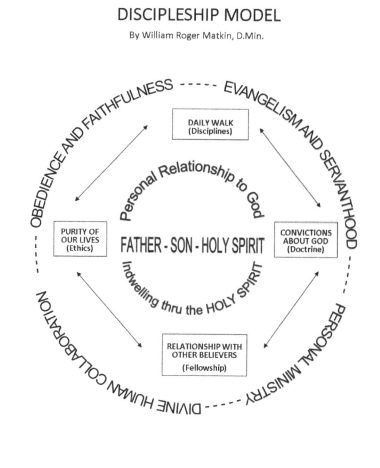

CHAPTER ONE

LAYING THE FOUNDATION: A NEW TESTAMENT PERSPECTIVE ON SPIRITUAL GROWTH

Spiritual growth is a modern construct for an ancient concept; it is a name for something that happens in the life of someone rightly related to God. In keeping with having a real and personal relationship with the Living God, a person can expect peace of heart and mind, a sense of purpose and genuine security in the face of the vagaries of life, and a movement from immaturity to maturity as one travels along life's journey. It is appropriate to give a name to that progressive journey – *spiritual growth*.

WORD STUDY

Let's take a look at those two words as well as other closely related words found in the New Testament. Somewhat ironically, the adjective *spiritual*, from the Greek, *pneumatik*, does not occur in any of the four Gospels.[1] The basic concept is there, but the actual word is not. As used elsewhere in the New Testament *spiritual* has the connotation of invisibility and power. The noun *growth* is from the Greek, *auxano,* and simply means *"to increase or become greater."* [2] The New Testament strongly supports the notion that spiritual growth is a natural dimension of Christian discipleship. In this chapter, our study of spiritual growth will be limited to several key ideas from the teachings of Jesus, and selective writings from the Apostles John, Peter, and Paul. Truth be known, the concept of spiritual growth is so pervasive in the New Testament that one can hardly open the pages without encountering, directly or indirectly, a related theme.

---

[1] Vine, W.E. An Expository Dictionary of New Testament Words. (Nashville: Thomas Nelson, 1985), p. 1077

[2] Thayer, Joseph Henry. A Greek-English Lexicon of the New Tesatament. (New York: Harper and Brothers, 1889), p. 84.

JESUS AND THE WORD 'DISCIPLE'

Jesus' use of the term *disciple* to describe his followers provides a firm foundation for this New Testament perspective on spiritual growth. From the Greek, *mathetes*, a disciple is *"one who accepts and follows a given teacher,"* [3] in this case, Jesus. The word occurs 260 times in the Gospels and Book of Acts, but nowhere else in the New Testament. It is used in three distinct ways: (1) referring to a follower of any great leader or movement, e.g. Matthew 22:16, John 9:28 (2) as the most frequently used term for believers in Christ (twenty-two times in Acts, e.g. 11:26, and numerous times in the Gospel of John, e.g. John 1:35-50, 7:3) (3) referring specifically to one or more of the Twelve Disciples of Jesus, e.g. Luke 9:54, John 6:8. [4]

JESUS AS TEACHER

It is quite clear from a cursory reading of the four Gospels that even the enemies of Jesus acknowledged his ministry as a teaching ministry, His teaching is a direct contradiction to their own. His followers were learning new ways of thinking about God. e.g., It was Jesus, the Teacher, who first used the Hebrew word, *Abba*, comparable to *Daddy* in modern English, to describe the Eternal God. That air of familiarity toward God infuriated the Jewish leaders. One of Jesus' main criticisms of the Pharisees was their unyielding dogmatism, intentional spiritual blindness, and their unwillingness to even consider a change. (Matthew 23:1-36) An obvious comparison between the disciples of Christ and the Pharisees was their respective attitudes toward personal spiritual growth. i.e. their openness to newness. As modern-day disciples of Jesus, it behooves us to share with our first-century predecessors an enthusiastic desire to embrace a lifelong pilgrimage of spiritual growth.

Jesus summarized the teaching-learning process when He said, " *A disciple is not above his teacher, but everyone, when he is fully taught, will be like his teacher"*. (Luke 6:40. RSV) In Jesus' day with no books, libraries, the

---

[3] Buttrick, G.A., Editor. Interpreter's Dictionary of the Bible. 4 vols. (New York: Abington Press, 1962), 1:844
[4] Ibid.,p.845

Internet, etc., it was impossible for a student to know more than his/her teacher. The best one could hope for was to be judged equal to his/her teacher. [5] Jesus highlights the limitless possibilities of a lifetime of learning from the Teacher, whose resources know no bounds. The *fully taught* disciple is the one *"on whom the teacher has exerted maximum influence."* [6] Helping you discover how to put yourself in the position with the Good Lord for Him to exert *maximum influence* is the goal of PUTTING IT ALL TOGETHER.

BECOMING LIKE CHILDREN

If change and spiritual growth are integrally related, then Jesus' teaching in Matthew 18:3 is a direct inference to his disciples' need for spiritual growth. He said, ". . . *unless you turn (RSV, change, TEV) and become like children, you will never enter the Kingdom of Heaven.*" RSV The Greek, *straphete*, simply means to *"turn, change one's direction."* The change suggested is comprehensive and would include one's daily habits, goals, lifestyle, etc. The irony here is that Jesus' teaching can be interpreted as *un-growth*, and *un-learning*. i.e. the normal human growth pattern is from childhood to adulthood. He is suggesting the very opposite, not in a general sense, but concerning certain characteristics of being a child. This is a good example of how Jesus' teaching is often counter-intuitive, turning well-accepted principles upside down. Jesus is saying that the new measure of greatness in his Kingdom is childlikeness, not to be confused with childishness. He is not so subtly suggesting that His ways are new ways, often counter-posing commonly accepted worldly wisdom and values, and that is why he phrased it as he did. He recognized that his disciples were headed in the wrong direction and unless they *turned* around they would be going away from the Kingdom of God, not toward it. His definition of spiritual growth was most likely a great revelation and surprise to his original disciple band.

---

[5] Morris, Leon. Tyndale New Testament Commentaries: The Gospel According to Luke. (Grand Rapids, Mich.:Eerdmans, 1974), p.133.
[6] Tolbert, Malcolm O. The Broadman Bible Commentary: Luke, 12 vols. (Nashville: Broadman Press, 1970),

The kind of spiritual growth suggested by Jesus is virtually impossible apart from Divine assistance. It has been said, *". . . the change that is necessary before a man becomes as a little child is not something he can bring about by himself . . . it is a new birth . . . supernatural in origin"* [7] When you think about it, that line of thinking corresponds to our everyday experience in the world of adults. So many people are prideful, some even arrogant, sorely lacking in the childlike humility which will be required for entrance into the Kingdom of God. In Jesus' day children, even more so than in our day, played an almost insignificant role in society, powerless and unnoticed. On one occasion Jesus was even scolded by his disciples when he paid *undue* attention to little children. Here's the scenario as found in the Gospel of Mark, 10:13-16:

> *"And they were bringing children to him, that he might touch them; and the disciples rebuked them. But when Jesus saw it he was indignant, and said to them (his disciples), 'Let the children come to me, do not hinder them; for to such belongs the Kingdom of God. Truly, I say to you, whoever does not receive the Kingdom of God like a child shall not enter it.' And he took them in his arms and blessed them, laying his hands upon them."* RSV

End of the discussion. Jesus' point was made clear. Relevant to our discussion about spiritual growth is that this *"becoming like a child"* does have a beginning with our *"new birth"*, but in truth, it has no ending per se. It is a journey that never ends in this life. In his prayer entitled, *"I Like Youngsters"*, Michel Quoist captures the message Jesus is trying to get across to his disciples. Following are poignant excerpts from this insightful prayer:

> God says: I like youngsters. I want people to be like them.
> I don't like old people unless they are still children.
> I want only children in my Kingdom; this has been decreed from the beginning of time.
> Youngsters—twisted, humped, wrinkled, white-bearded- all kinds of youngsters, but youngsters.
> There is no changing it; it has been decided. There is room for no one else.

---

[7] Tasker, R.V.G. Tyndale New Testament Commentaries: The Gospel According to Matthew. (Grand Rapids, Mich.: Eerdmans, 1961), p. 175.

I like them because they are still growing, they are still improving.
They are on the road, they are on their way.
But with grown-ups there is nothing to expect anymore.
They will no longer grow, no longer improve.
They have come to full stop.
It is disastrous – grown-ups thinking they have arrived.
Alleluia! Alleluia! Open, all of you, little old men!
It is I, your God, the Eternal, risen from the dead,
coming to bring to life the child in you.
Hurry, Now is the time. I am ready to give you again the beautiful
face of a child, the beautiful eyes of a child. For I love youngsters,
and I want everyone to be like them.[i] (Michel Quoist, Prayers)[8]

THE APOSTLE PAUL ON SPIRITUAL GROWTH

No one captured the mind of Christ regarding spiritual growth better than
the Apostle Paul. We will look at four passages from his writings as
representative of the whole. Transformation is the theme of Romans
12:2:

> *"Do not be conformed to this world but be transformed by the*
> *renewal of your mind, that you may prove what is the will of God,*
> *what is good, acceptable and perfect."* RSV

To some extent every one of us begins our journey as a follower of Jesus
as conformed to the world in which we have lived; it is impossible to do
otherwise. We are inevitably shaped by our social, moral, intellectual, and
religious environment. *Conformed* is from the Greek root, *schema*, which
refers to a person's outward form which is continuously changing. We
look different when we are ten years old than we do at seventy.[9] True,
but that is hardly his point. It is with our inner self that Paul is concerned
because that too has been *"conformed to this world"*.

It is our proclivity to conformation which necessitates transformation.
From the Greek, *metamorphusthai*, the word implies a total reorientation
of life. The root word is *morphe* which means the essential unchanging
shape or element of anything.[10] This is in direct contrast with *schema*. In

---

[8] Quoist, Michel. Prayers. (Kansas City: Sheed and Ward, 1963), pp. 3-5.
[9] Barclay, William. Daily Bible Study Series: The Letters to the Romans.
(Philadelphia: Westminster Press, 1955),.167.
[10] Ibid.

11

changing these words, Paul is saying that becoming a genuine disciple of Jesus Christ involves a change in the core of our being, rather than a mere token change in our outward form.[11] However, a serious-minded reorientation inside will inevitably precipitate outward changes in our habits, preferences, conversation, etc. The medium of transformation is the *"renewal of our mind"*. *Renewal* is the English translation of the Greek, *anakainos*, meaning to make new in character and essential nature, to renovate and make qualitatively new.[12]

Biblical scholars part ways regarding the agency of this renewal, some leaning more toward the Holy Spirit at work in the believer, and others focused more on the human side of the equation, i.e. the believer becomes the agent of change via the regular practice of the classical spiritual disciplines of prayer, serious-minded Bible study, etc. which are presented in this book in great detail. The truth? Squarely in the middle of these two sides. As always, the Divine-human partnership is the way God works in the lives of his children from antiquity to the present. The Scripture, Old and New Testament, bears bold witness to that reality for those whose eyes are opened to see and understand spiritual truths.

II Corinthians 3:18 carries the theme of transformation a step further and focuses squarely on the Divine dimension of spiritual growth. It reads as follows in two classic translations of the Holy Scripture:

> *"And we all with unveiled face, beholding the glory of the Lord,* ***are being changed*** *into his likeness from one degree of glory to another; for* ***this comes from the Lord*** *who is the Spirit."* RSV
> *"But all of us who are Christians have no veils on our faces, but reflect like mirrors the glory of the Lord.* ***We are transfigured*** *in ever-increasing splendor into his own image, and* ***the transformation comes from the Lord*** *who is the Spirit."* J.B Phillips translation

If there were only this verse from which to formulate a doctrine of spiritual growth, one would have to conclude that the Divine element is the critical one. There are various nuances in the translation of this verse from Greek, but unanimous agreement on the main point which is that God Himself is the Transformer, and the Divine Agency of that

---

[11] Ibid.
[12] Vine, Ibid., p.950.

transformation is God's Spirit. The only hint of human participation is in the *"beholding"* as translated in the RSV. The regular keeping of the classical spiritual disciplines is the practical means of *"beholding the glory of the Lord"* for the believer.

The next phrase, **". . . *are being changed* . . ."**, translates the Greek verb *metamorphoumetha*, which is essentially the same word translated *"transformed"* in Romans 12:2. One of the great Reformers during the Protestant Reformation, John Calvin (1509-1564 AD) wrote this in his Commentary on II Corinthians 3:18 concerning this change or transformation resulting in spiritual growth:

> "(Spiritual growth is) . . . not accomplished in us in one moment, *but we must be constantly making progress* both in the knowledge of God, and in conformity to His image . . . . The design of the Gospel is this – that the image of God may be stamped anew upon us, and that the advancement of this restoration *may be continually going forward in us during our whole life,* because God makes his glory shine forth in us little by little . . ." [13]

It is abundantly clear that spiritual growth was no foreign theme to the great reformer of Geneva. From his understanding of the New Testament Calvin testifies to the progressive nature of spiritual growth, to the Divine impetus, and hints at the human aspect. For him, spiritual growth involved both the intellect (*knowledge of God*) and one's character (*conformity to the image of God*).

In summary, Paul teaches in II Corinthians 3:18 that spiritual growth is produced by the creative power of the Holy Spirit, not human effort, even as a plant grows merely by *thrusting forth* its leaves into the sunlight. However, in keeping with the underlying theme of this book, intentionality, the *thrusting forth* requires self-discipline and effort which becomes the means of contact with the Spirit Who produces the positive change, aka, spiritual growth. [14] So the paradox remains intact - spiritual growth is simultaneously the product of Divine power and human cooperation.

---

[13] Pringle, John, translator. <u>Calvin's Commentaries.</u> vol.11. (Edinburgh: Calvin Translation Society, 1954), p.187
14 Reid, James. <u>Interpreter's Bible.</u> 10:313,314.

The Apostle Paul's emphasis in Ephesians 4:13-15 is on the corporate dimension of spiritual growth. He writes:

> ". . . *until we all attain to the unity of the faith and of the knowledge of the Son of God, to* **mature manhood,** *to the measure of* **the stature of the fullness of Christ;** *so that we may* **no longer be children,** *tossed to and fro and carried about with every wind of doctrine, by the cunning of men, by their craftiness in deceitful wiles. Rather,* **speaking the truth** *in love, we are* **to grow up in every way** *into him who is the head, into Christ . . .".*
> RSV

Throughout this passage Paul uses the first person plural pronoun, *we.* The main point is the growth and maturation of the Body of Christ, the Church universal. The correlation is simply that the Body of Christ matures as its members mature.

Full participation in the common life of a Christian fellowship (for most folks, a local church of some flavor) is often an effective means of moving toward personal maturity. My Greek and New Testament professor in seminary, Curtis Vaughan, said it well, "*The goal is for the whole company of the redeemed to reach maturity. The idea is not mainly that of individual believers attaining to perfection, rather the Church, viewed as a single organism, reaching its spiritual stature.*" [15]

Several key phrases in this passage are pertinent and worthy of our investigation. "*Mature manhood*" (RSV) and "*the measure of the stature of the fullness of Christ*" (RSV) are parallel in meaning and lift up the goal of spiritual growth. And a lofty goal it is! It is one that should hold our attention for a lifetime. It is also noteworthy that Paul juxtaposes a call to spiritual maturity against a warning not to remain children because of the actual challenges posed by "*cunning, crafty, and deceitful*" adversaries that potentially would lead them astray morally and doctrinally (*their belief system*). The only way to avoid dangerous spiritual influences, which potentially derail us, is by continuous spiritual growth. [16] Most commentators connect "*in love*" with "*speaking the truth*". This simple criterion, "*in love*", is an important reminder that in Christian

---

[15] Vaughan, W. Curtis. The Letter to the Ephesians. (Nashville: Convention Press, 1963), p. 92

[16] Barclay, William. Daily Bible Study Series: The Letters to the Galatians and Ephesians. (Philadelphia: Westminster, 1976),p. 151.

relationships, honesty must always be tempered by love, which is at the top of the pyramid of Christian virtues. I Corinthians 13, one of the most quoted passages in all of the Bible, often titled the Love Chapter, strongly defends this principle. However, it is in the context of an honest and truthful Christian fellowship (Greek, *koinonia*) that personal spiritual growth most readily occurs.

That's exactly what happened to me during my four years at Texas A&M. The Lord brought into my life a small group of young men who shared a passion for the Lord, and a deep desire to know him and to grow as young Christians. There was a level of transparency with those guys I had not known before. Our experience was reflected in the title of a recently published book at that time by Keith Miller entitled, <u>The Taste of New Wine</u>. [17] The *new wine* was our experience of *koinonia*, genuine fellowship in the Lord at a level none of us ever tasted before. It was intoxicating, metaphorically speaking. For a couple of years during that time at A&M, we met a couple of nights a week at the Baptist Student Center. It was not a program scheduled by anyone but our small group. I was on the leadership team for the Baptist Student Union and had the keys to the building. It was my responsibility to make certain the building was locked when our meeting was over and it was usually late at night. We had no official ending time. The guys in that group remain today my friends in Christ.

After about four years of marriage in the early '1970s, my wife and I had a similarly transforming small group experience at Broadway Baptist Church in Ft. Worth, Texas where I was serving as a Baptist Campus minister at three local campuses. We participated in a Yokefellow group the purpose of which was personal spiritual growth and the bonus of which was growth in our marriage. The weekly format included introspection, un-coerced sharing of our needs with the group, and prayer together. We faced our *demons* and received honest feedback from the group members. It was a very powerful experience and one I treasure to this very day.

Back to the Scripture at hand, Ephesians 4:13-15. "... *grow up in every way unto Him"* requires that believers serve as mirrors for each other, sharing honest feedback in a spirit of genuine love and concern. That kind of *mutual edification* (building up) is key to personal spiritual growth. The beauty of Paul's thought in this passage is his marriage of personal

---

[17] Miller, Keith. The Taste of New Wine. (Waco: Word Books, 1965)

spiritual growth with the corporate growth of the Body of Christ, which is the Church (in the universal sense of that word). This message is a necessary corrective for any Christian leader or individual believer who tends to elevate the individual spiritual experience to unhealthy extremes.

In Colossians 2:6,7, Paul comes closest to tipping the balance toward the human side of the spiritual growth equation. All four metaphors used by Paul in this passage involve direct human agency. The Divine dimension is present, but only by way of implication rather than explicit teaching.

> "As therefore you **received** Christ Jesus the Lord, so **live** in Him, **rooted** and **built up** in Him and **established** in the faith, just as you were **taught**, abounding in **thanksgiving**." RSV

"Received" is from the Greek "paralambano", which literally means, to receive from another, or to receive something transmitted.[18] In this case, the transmitter was Epaphras (see Colossians 1:7,8), Paul's beloved fellow servant and minister of Christ. Paul is simply encouraging the Colossian believers to stay on the path of discipleship laid out by Epaphras. The initial and pivotal action for the new Christian is to receive Christ into one's heart. Everything changes after that, or at least should change. The Greek, "peripatein", is rendered live or walk in various New Testament translations and refers to the whole tenor of a person's daily existence.[19] In these verses, there is an appeal to consistency, and continuity, from the past to the present, "as you received … so live". The Apostle Paul reveals his concern in these verses for spiritual nurture as well as evangelism. In a more general sense, what happens after conversion is the focus of much of his writing to the churches.

"Rooted" (rhizeodomeo), "built up" (epoikodomeo), and "established" (bebaiomenoi) translate three Greek participles which provide very helpful metaphors of the developing Christian life. "'Rooted" provides the picture of a growing plant. The verb is a perfect participle that refers to something which occurred in the past, but whose effects endure to the present. As a lifetime gardener, I thoroughly understand the picture being painted by Paul. When you pull up a healthy tomato plant at the end of the season from which dozens of tomatoes have been picked, you'll find, under the surface, a huge root system that continuously fed the plant throughout the growing season. "Built up" refers to a building under

---

[18] Thayer, Ibid.,p.484.
[19] Beare, Francis W., Interpreter's Bible, 11:188

construction; it is a present participle, implying steady growth and development. The prepositional phrase *"in Him"* suggests that Christ is the essential means by which the structure of the building is held together. [20] *"Established"*, another present participle, has the connotation of *"continuous strengthening"*. [21] Each of the three metaphors strongly supports the idea of spiritual growth as an integral part of Christian discipleship, and because of the nature of these metaphors in the Greek language, also places significant responsibility for spiritual growth squarely on the shoulders of the individual. These verses end on a note of thanksgiving to God born of true humility which recognizes that all spiritual growth is ultimately from God.[22]

If Jesus had any *best friends* among the Twelve, Peter, James, and John would be those men. It was that trio that Jesus invited to be with him on the Mount of Transfiguration (Matthew 17:1-13). They knew Jesus well and played prominent roles in the content of the New Testament. We will end our brief New Testament perspective on Christian discipleship/spiritual growth with selected passages from the writings of Peter and John.

THE APOSTLE PETER ON SPIRITUAL GROWTH

> *"God's divine power has given us everything we need to live a truly religious life through our knowledge of the one who called us to share in his own glory and goodness.*
> *In this way he has given us the very great and precious gifts he promised, so that by means of these gifts you may escape from the destructive lust that is in the world, and may come to share the divine nature."* II Peter 1:3, 4 (TEV)

What a beautiful promise this is! None of us start our journey of discipleship as fully developed men and women of spiritual maturity. It is indeed a lifelong process that ends with our *"sharing the divine nature"*! II Peter 3:18 is the very last verse of Peter's concise letter addressed to a wide circle of early Christians. He ends his letter on the same theme as he begins it in chapter I.

---

[20] Carson, Herbert M. Tyndale New Testament Commentary: The Epistle of Paul to the Colossians. (Grand Rapids, Mich.:Eerdmans,1960), p.60
[21] Ibid.
[22] Carson, Ibid.p.61

"But continue to grow in the grace and knowledge of our Lord and Savior Jesus Christ. To Him be the glory, now and forever!"

For Peter, the Christian life involves development as we progressively get to know the person of God in Christ at greater and greater depths. There is never an arrival for the true Christian. If we ever stop moving on the road of discipleship we are in trouble, even as the rider of a bicycle would be. [23]

It is noteworthy that Peter, who knew Christ from the very beginning of his public ministry and followed Him in faithful discipleship throughout his adult life, would come to the conclusion in his final years on this earth that spiritual growth is at the very heart of Christian discipleship.

THE APOSTLE JOHN

John, who might well have known Jesus even better than Peter, came to similar conclusions. He used different language to express his views on spiritual growth, but he certainly highlighted the idea of growth in his brief letter of I John.

> He said in I John 3:2, *"Beloved we are God's children now; it does not yet appear what we shall be, but we know that when He appears, we shall be like Him, for we shall see Him as He is."* RSV

In John's mind *"becoming like Him"* cannot be postponed to the future life . . . the change begins already in this life.[24] For John, one of Jesus' best friends, sonship, being a child of God, is not a mere title or doctrine. It is not static but dynamic. A child of God grows, develops, matures, and the goal of that growth is maturity in the *likeness of Christ Himself.*[25] John sounds a clear note concerning the endpoint of spiritual growth. He understands that since conversion the Father through the agency of the Holy Spirit has been transforming each of his children into the likeness of his Son Jesus.[26] That beautiful, difficult, mysterious, paradoxical transformation is definitely on the asset side of the ledger in the Christian's economy of things.

---

[23] Green, Michael. <u>Tyndale New Testament Commentaries: The Second Epistle General of Peter</u>. (Grand Rapids, Mich: Erdmans, 1968), p.150.

[24] Wilder, Amos N., <u>Interpreters Bible</u>. 12:254-255.

[25] McDowell, Edward A., <u>Broadmans Bible Commentary,</u> 12:207.

[26] Stott, J.R.W. <u>Tyndale New Testament Commentary: The Epistles of John.</u> (Grand Rapids,Mich.:Eerdmans,1960),p119.

At the end of this *New Testament Perspective on Spiritual Growth*, I share the feelings of the Apostle John expressed at the end of his Gospel when he said:

> *"But there are also many other things which Jesus did; were every one of them to be written, I suppose that the world itself could not contain the books that would be written."* John 21:25 RSV

Well --- there are many more New Testament passages to be examined on the subject of spiritual growth, but this book *"cannot contain them"*!

CONCLUSION

The New Testament affirms in many and various ways that spiritual growth is an important aspect of God's design for his children. He provides motivation and has revealed the means for personal growth. It remains an individual matter for each child of God to act on that motivation and avail himself/herself of the means.

CHAPTER TWO

THE INDWELLING AND ABIDING LIFE

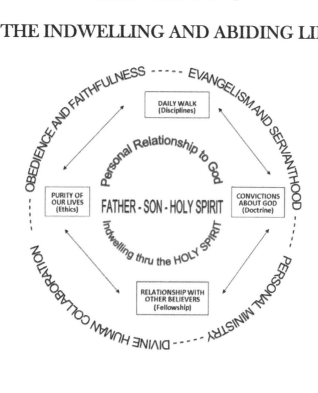

A Christian is not simply someone affiliated with a particular religion; at the very heart of it, a Christian is someone who has **a Personal Relationship with the living God**. It's that simple; it's that complicated. All the pertinent references in Scripture point to that reality. Anything short of that is missing the whole point of Jesus' life and message.

In Matthew 22:37 Jesus says it straight out in answer to a question regarding the *"greatest commandment"*. His answer, *"Love the Lord your God with all your heart, with all your soul, and with all your mind."* TEV Jesus' answer does not reflect a legal agreement between a person and God, rather he uses a verb that is used universally in the context of significant relationships.

THE GOSPEL OF JOHN

From the outset of John's Gospel, the Divine/human relationship is familial. *"Some however did receive him (Jesus) and believed in Him; so he gave them the right to become God's children. They did not become God's children by natural means, that is by being born as the children of a human father; God himself was their Father."* John 1:12,13 (TEV) In a healthy family parents love their children and vice versa.

John *records* the following poignant words of Jesus at the very beginning of what has been called his *Priestly Prayer* in John 17:1-3. This prayer was prayed on the very last night of his life in the Garden of Gethsemane. He would be crucified the very next day. It would seem reasonable to conclude that his words were well-chosen and of particular significance. The prayer comprises the entire chapter, all twenty-six verses, but these three verses set the stage for what is to follow. *"1 Father, the hour has come. Give glory to your Son, so that the Son may give glory to You. 2 For You gave Him authority over all mankind so that He might give eternal life to all those You gave Him. 3 And eternal life means to know You, the only true God, and to know Jesus Christ whom you sent."* (TEV)

There are so, so many beautiful promises in God's Word about every aspect of our lives, but concerning this conversation about the **Indwelling/Abiding Life**, there is one in particular that for the past three or four years has captured my imagination and my attention. It reads as follows:

"Jesus answered him, 'Whoever loves me will obey my teaching. My Father will love him, and my Father and I will come to him and live with him.'" John 14:23 (TEV)

Permit me to share with you this verse in several other translations, including the original Greek text:

The literal Greek translation is somewhat fascinating here. *"Answered Jesus and said to him, if anyone loves me, the word of me he will keep and the Father of me will love him and to him, we will come and a home with him will make."*

"And to this Jesus replied, 'When a man loves me, he follows my teaching. Then my Father will love him, and we will come to that man and make our home within him.'" John 14:23
(J.B. Phillips Translation)

22

"Jesus replied, 'If anyone loves me, he will obey my teaching. My Father will love him, and <u>we will come to him and make our home with him</u>.'" John 14:23 (NIV)

THE APOSTLE PAUL'S WRITINGS

The Apostle Paul *gets it* as he writes in Philippians 3:8-10, *". . . I reckon everything as a complete loss for the sake of what is so much more valuable, <u>the knowledge of Christ Jesus my Lord</u>. For his sake I have thrown everything away; I consider it all as mere garbage, so that I may gain Christ and <u>be completely united with him</u> . . . <u>All I want is to know Christ</u>, and to experience the power of his resurrection, to share in his sufferings and become like him in his death, in the hope that I myself will be raised from death to life."* (TEV)

GOD AS THREE IN ONE

The **Indwelling and Abiding life** inevitably involves a discussion of the nature of God, specifically, the Trinity. Paul's benediction in II Corinthians 13:14 is one of about twenty verses in the New Testament that has all three Persons of the Trinity listed together. It reads as follows: *"The grace of the **Lord Jesus Christ,** the love of **God,** and the fellowship of the **Holy Spirit** be with you all."* (TEV) Matthew 28:19 is one of the more familiar verses: *"Go therefore and make disciples of all nations, baptizing them in the name of the Father and the Son and the Holy Spirit . . .".* (RSV) Difficult to explain, harder to understand, God as Three-in-One is central to the revelation of Scripture. The analogy inevitably falls short but thinking of God and history as a screenplay is somewhat helpful. Suppose we divide all of human history into three parts as revealed in Scripture. **Act One** of the play as described in the Old Testament portrays **God the Father** as occupying front and center stage; Act **Two** coincides with the New Testament, the four Gospels specifically, with **Jesus, the Son of God**, his birth, life, and resurrection as the primary focus; finally, **Act Three begins** with the Ascension of Jesus, as described in the Book of Acts, followed by the coming of the **Holy Spirit** who becomes the focus. In each "Act," all three Persons are a present reality. e.g. Jesus was described as the *"maker of all things"*. And all through the Old Testament, the Spirit of God is referred to countless times. Another helpful word that is sometimes used to describe the Trinity is the *"Godhead"*, used by William Tyndale in his translation of the Bible in 1525 AD.

Whatever term we come up with to describe the Triune God, they all describe (point to) the same **Reality**. And it is that **Divine Reality** in Whom we *abide*, and Who **indwells** us, *"makes his home in us!"*

IMPLICATIONS OF THE INDWELLING AND ABIDING LIFE

Let's assume that knowing and loving God is the norm for Christians of all time. As His children that would be our natural inclination. If so, what does that mean in a practical sense? i.e. how do we spend the twenty-four hours allotted to mankind for each day of our lives?

One of the obvious characteristics of a loving relationship is the intense desire to spend time together. Could be friend to friend, husband to wife . . . . It is an observable principle that people who love each other want to spend time together. You have already figured out where I'm going with this line of thought.

Administer a self-test. Simply answer the question. *"Do my daily habits demonstrate a desire to spend time with God, one on One?"* You say you "love" Him, just how is that love lived out in your daily/weekly schedule? On numerous occasions I've been told something like this: "On *my morning commute, that's when I pray and commune with God."* Pardon me, but it seems to me that is an insult to Him! *"I have nothing else to do, so I'll pray."* Ok, I'm not saying that's not possible or even a decent idea, but in my opinion, that approach falls way short of what God expects of his daughters and sons. Would that level of fellowship work in a truly loving relationship? No, it would not. So who are you fooling? Not, God, that's for sure. Yourself? Most likely.

EXAMINE YOUR HEART

The first step in remedying this situation is to examine your heart. The Wisdom of Solomon from the book of Proverbs affirms this form of self-examination.

> *"Keep your heart with all vigilance, for from it flows the springs of life."* Proverbs 4:23 RSV

The NIV translation is a bit less poetic, and more to the point.

> *"Above all else, guard your heart, for everything else you do flows from it."*

So the pertinent question becomes, *"Do I know and love God as Father and Son?" "Does my current life substantiate that assertion? What needs to change in my life?"* The practical implications of maintaining a **Relationship with God** are addressed in detail in Chapter Three, *"The Daily Walk"*. Initially, however, your most important assignment is to ascertain the reality and true nature of your **Relationship with God**.

TO WHAT END?

You may be asking yourself a question like this, *"The Indwelling and Abiding* "sounds good, maybe it is, but for what purpose, what result, and what is the goal per se?" This is a good question indeed and the answer is readily available in Scripture, specifically the New Testament. Jesus, in His *"Sermon on the Mount"* (Gospel of Matthew, Chapters 5,6,7), describes in great detail the nature of the Kingdom of God and the kind of folks who will be part of that Kingdom, sons, and daughters of the Most High God, the Father, and disciples of his Blessed Son, Jesus. They will be the kind of people He described as *"salt and light"*, who are peacemakers, meek, show mercy, pure in heart, and suffer persecution ...... Children of God's Kingdom will learn how to handle anger, honor their marriage vows, turn the other cheek, and not only love their friends and family but also their enemies! As part of his discussion on who you are to love,

Jesus said,

> "You have heard that it was said, 'Love your friends, hate your enemies.' But now I tell you: love your enemies, and pray for those who mistreat you, so that you will become the sons of your Father in heaven. For He makes his sun to shine on bad and good people alike, and gives rain to those who do right and those who do wrong. Why should you expect God to reward you, if you love only the people who love you? Even the tax collectors do that! And if you speak only to your friends, have you done anything out of the ordinary? Even the pagans do that! You must be perfect – just as your Father in heaven is perfect." Matthew 5:43-48 TEV

Jesus said that with a straight face and He meant it! *"Impossible"*, you say. In God's economy, possible indeed! Improbable maybe, but very possible, even for redeemed sinners like you and me. That, you see, is the endpoint, the goal of **the indwelling and the abiding life**, this lifelong journey of being a disciple of Jesus. Jesus, the Teacher, said in Luke 6:40, **"No pupil is greater than his teacher; but every pupil, when he has completed his training, will be like his teacher."** That, my friend in Christ, is what **PIAT** is all about. There is nothing easy or simple about the process, but the payoff is tremendous!

CHAPTER THREE

THE DAILY WALK

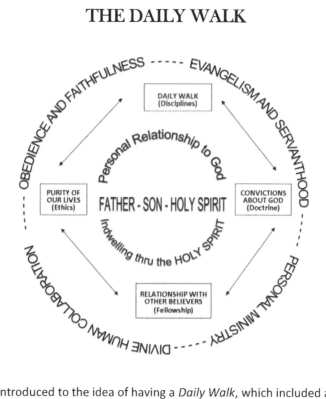

I was introduced to the idea of having a *Daily Walk*, which included a *Quiet Time*, as a freshman at Texas A&M in the fall of 1963. I was involved in two complimentary Christian organizations that year, Baptist Student Union and the Navigators. Ultimately I had to choose between the two as they were quite different in terms of focus and intensity. The *Navs* were unlike anything to which I had ever been exposed. The leader, Bill Gibbs, was an ex-Marine, and very intense. As could be expected his focus was discipline in the areas of having a daily quiet time, memorizing Scripture, and personal evangelism on campus. After 57 years or so, I never forgot one of his quotes and it impacted my practice of campus ministry for the forty-one years I was privileged to do it. It went something like this: *"If you play a man's game, men will come to play."* I came out of a typical Baptist church background where the youth ministry seemed to be predominately female and centered around Youth Choir. Well . . . I was not inclined in that direction so was not interested or impressed.

Throughout my career in campus ministry, I tried my best to have a program that would be attractive to both young men and women. The goal was a healthy, balanced approach. And it worked!

Each of my four years at Texas A&M was life-changing. I embraced the disciplines of a daily walk including quiet times and Scripture memory, but I had to be creative to make it happen. As a freshman member of the Corps of Cadets, I lived in a Corps dorm with a roommate in a room the size of a large closet. Our wake-up call every morning was by bugle at 6:00 am. We had to be downstairs fully dressed and standing at attention by 6:30 am if I remember correctly. The bottom line: with a room that small and a roommate and that schedule, an early morning quiet Time was not possible. Those were the days when 18 semester hours was the normal load for Engineering students, and included courses in Chemistry, Physics, Mathematics, and Engineering, with labs for each course. My schedule was packed so I had to be very intentional about finding a time slot to have quiet time to be with the Lord, but I did. Sometimes it happened in the library, crowded yet private, or on a bench outside under an oak tree, and often in the All Faiths Chapel right in the middle of campus. Remember Proverbs 4:23, *"Keep your heart with all vigilance, for from it flow the springs of life."*(RSV) My intentional efforts reflected my heart's longing for time with the Lord. A brand new thing for me. During my Junior year, I read Keith Miller's book, The Taste of New Wine. I lapped it up. It perfectly described what was going on in my life in my relationship with God. I was in fact "tasting new wine" and I loved it. Thus began my lifelong journey of *intentionally* having a daily walk, and a quiet time. That was 1963-67 and now 55 years later I'm 77, still at it, and doing a better job for the most part. For the last 35 years or so I've gotten up at about 5:15 am, have my morning cup(s) of Folgers, and done my thing with the Lord.

But . . . I have not always been that consistent. I've had a few *dry* times, and one in particular, required a tragic event to get me back in the harness. I was about 40 years old when my father died of a heart attack in our living room with my family watching – my Mom, wife, and our two children. My Dad's death was hard enough, expected since he had a serious case of heart disease, but losing him was still difficult. But even harder was settling his affairs in such a way as to provide a living for my mother who was 60 at the time. It would not be appropriate for me to include the particulars in this setting, but suffice it to say his business affairs were a mess. One *deal* in particular in his last days did not pan out and he was left with a substantial amount of debt and limited assets to satisfy those debts. As executor of his estate, it was my role to settle his affairs, and with the help of my two younger brothers, we were able to do so, but it took about five years.

I will tell one story because it's both tragic and funny at the same time. My Mom and Dad owned a large mobile home park and a dilapidated sewer treatment plant that served the residents. For years I had begged him to take care of the sewer plant, sell it, give it away, whatever. He did not do so, and then he died. The management and maintenance of the sewer plant were shared by my brother and me. The *pits* were 15' deep, with straight-up walls, and filled with . . . well, you can guess what they were filled with. One day when I was doing some maintenance I came close to falling into one of the pits. I was by myself. If I had fallen in I likely would have drowned in the sewage. So when I see the bumper sticker, ". . . . . . *happens*." I take it personally because "*it*" almost happened to me literally and figuratively. The end of the sewer plant story was that our family *paid* the local municipality to *buy* our sewer plant. That was one very unique transaction!

At the front end of my journey as executor of my dad's estate, it became clear to me that this was a mountain that would be difficult to climb with our family resources. To be perfectly honest, up to that point in my life I had handled virtually every challenge life had thrown at me. That may sound absurd and arrogant, but I'm speaking the truth. Now in some ways for the first time, I realized this was an unsolvable problem without Divine assistance. So I began in earnest to seek His help and wisdom, and so renewed again my commitment to an early morning quiet time. I made it my aim to rise an hour before my family, so about 5:15 am. That was about 35 years ago; I *enjoyed* that discipline so much that I have continued doing it to this very day.

Back to the business at hand - our daily walk with God. About 10 years after my Dad died, I had my own brush with death. I was forty-nine years old, overweight, had high blood pressure, high cholesterol . . . a walking time bomb of sorts. One Sunday morning I left our house for a walk, got about two blocks from our house, and began having classic left arm pain, i.e. angina.   I turned around and went back to the house. Monday I set out on my walk again, hoping the angina was an aberration. As with the day before, the arm pain happened again. I made an appointment with a cardiologist and was diagnosed with early-onset, severe, aggressive coronary artery disease. On Friday of that week, I had angioplasty to remove the blockage in two vessels, one was 95% blocked. So began my journey with heart disease. In the ensuing 27 years, I have had three more interventions, with five stents in place and I am *healthy* according to my doctor. That will put the *fear of God* in you. Over the years I became more and more serious about my daily exercise regimen, literally my "daily walk" for very good reasons, my well-being, and long-term health. In fact, after my last intervention, my cardiologist told me that I likely would not have survived the procedure if I had not been in *good shape* . . . gratifying news to hear.

So what's the point of my sharing these personal experiences? Because there is a direct correlation between our physical and spiritual well-being. If you neglect the spiritual disciplines espoused in this book it will be to your detriment. There are simply no shortcuts to a vibrant, healthy, happy, fruitful life as a disciple of Jesus.

What is one's *daily walk* with God supposed to look like? The answer: There is no set pattern, no right way to do it. There is no wrong way if it is working for you. Here are some basic ideas and guidelines. What makes the most sense concerning timing is at the very front end of your day. That is the point in the day when your mind is the least cluttered with the busyness of life. At minimum allow yourself thirty uncluttered minutes for your quiet time. Develop a routine that includes reflection, a defined regimen of Scripture reading, and prayer. For example, sequentially reading through the Old Testament and New Testament simultaneously and also one Psalm per day. After completing the Psalms (150 chapters, so five months of daily reading) consider using Proverbs 30 chapters, one month's reading) in the same manner. In essence, I'm suggesting a Bible *sandwich* daily with an OT and NT chapter on each end and a chapter from the Psalms or Proverbs in the middle. If this sounds like too much for you to handle, then do less. My observation is that most folks have never read through the Bible, Old or New Testament. If you feel like you have to choose between the two, then choose the New Testament, beginning with the Gospel of Matthew, and then on through the other three Gospels, Paul's letters, etc. Remember this is a lifetime project. Do not be discouraged. You have the rest of your life! In addition to Scripture, there are other classic books as supplemental options for devotional reading (see *PRACTICAL TOOLS and RELATED MATERIALS, VIII SUGGESTED READING*, p. 122). But my focus here is your engagement with the Bible, not books that others have written about the message of Scripture.

Quiet Time will include your prayers, oral and possibly written prayers that can dovetail with keeping a spiritual journal. (see *PRACTICAL TOOLS and RELATED MATERIALS, I SPIRITUAL JOURNAL*, p. 87) Prayer is nothing more or less than "*. . . pouring out your heart to God . . .*" (Psalm 62:8 RSV). As mentioned above some folks prefer to write out their daily prayers in journal fashion, others predominately verbal. Daily prayers inevitably include petitions and intercessions, i.e. we live in a world that is full of challenges, questions, and problems. Jesus said it best in John 16:33. "*I have told you these things so that in me you may have perfect peace and confidence. In the world, you have tribulations and trials and distress and frustration, but be of good cheer for I have overcome the world. I have deprived it of power to harm, have conquered it for you.*" (Amplified New Testament) You will find specific recommendations for your prayer life in *PRACTICAL TOOLS and RELATED MATERIALS*, V. QUIET TIME, p. 115.

Included in the idea of establishing a daily routine is having a special place for your quiet time. For many, the choices might be limited, for others not so much. The familiarity of place and routine is a powerful elixir for steadying one's life in a chaotic world. My routine includes a special chair that comes out of my wife's family and a fresh-brewed cup of Folgers coffee. You may prefer tea . . . as they say in Spanish, "*no le hace*". It doesn't matter one whit. This is your quiet time, you get to set the routine and pick the beverage of choice! If this is a new discipline for you, get ready for a pleasant surprise. You'll be going to bed looking forward to the new day and special time with the Lord.

CHAPTER FOUR

OUR CONVICTIONS ABOUT GOD
WHAT WE BELIEVE

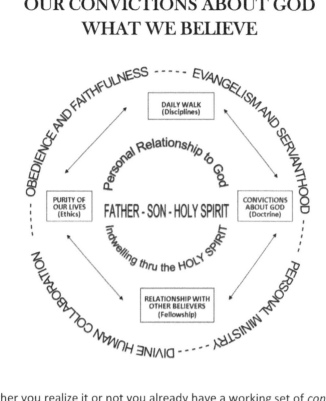

Whether you realize it or not you already have a working set of *convictions* about God, life, marriage, money, work, morals . . . They may need to be upgraded, changed, amended, corrected, tweaked a bit, or expanded, but they are already in place. And it is from that *place* that you are living.

Since you already have a basic set of beliefs about God, it is important to examine them and see how they compare to orthodox Christian beliefs that have crystallized over millennia, e.g., the Apostles Creed is a good example of what I am alluding to.

This is not to say that there exists a *gold standard* regarding what is *orthodox* Christian belief. The various denominations of Christian churches – Protestant/Catholic, and liberal/conservative serve as good examples. And even within a particular denomination there is a spectrum of beliefs about God, and ethics, e.g., in the Baptist world with which I am most familiar, there is the Southern Baptist Convention (conservative), the Cooperative Baptist Fellowship (liberal), as well as other groups with a variety of doctrines. This may be confusing to you, but it is simple to understand that every believer needs to come to his/her own set of basic beliefs about God, the Bible, morality . . . , then you can figure out where you might most naturally *fit* in a church setting. I was *born and raised* in a traditional Southern Baptist church, but at this point in my life, I do not fit that mold very well. Not only has the SBC changed rather dramatically, but so have I. Over the decades, the passage of time has a way of refining your preferences for styles of preaching, music, worship styles, etc. But that's not a problem as there are no hard and fast rules along those lines. What is important is for you to line up with what God has revealed to you in Scripture about Himself and the way things are supposed to be in matters of religion and morality. With that in mind, it can still be a bit confusing because various opinions will always exist regarding the interpretation of Scripture.

The first step is to ascertain your basic convictions about the Scripture itself: whether or not it will be your *guiding light*, and whether or not it is authoritative and foundational. Once you have come to the point of putting Scripture in its proper place, you have made a huge step forward in your quest to formulate your basic belief system. It is no easy matter even from that perspective, but it is possible and quite frankly, necessary that you do so.

When you think about the storyline of the Old Testament right from the start, you might surmise that the challenge faced by Almighty God was to re-set the image folks had fixed in their minds about Him. Jesus had the same challenge – to enlighten the common misconceptions about the Eternal God, His Father. Over the centuries the Jewish hierarchy had it all wrong. Jesus' teaching, his sermons, parables, and the Model Prayer had the effect of making his hearers examine their *beliefs about God* because they were *dead* wrong in most cases of any significance. Here are a few obvious examples: social status does not equal spiritual vitality, the significance of outward appearance versus inward purity, and wealth versus poverty as signs of God's approval/disapproval. For the Twelve, his inner circle, he had to clarify in their minds that spiritual privilege is dis-associated with *leader* versus servant of all, a concept virtually incomprehensible to them. The one who serves is presented by Jesus as *greater* in God's estimation than the one being served. A radical idea indeed! The Twelve had that all wrong!

My purpose in this chapter is not to come up with a new *Matkin Creed* for the 21st Century, but to highlight the necessity for every believer, and every child of God to have a correct, solid, enlightened understanding of God, His Son, Jesus, and the Holy Spirit, based entirely on the Biblical revelation (Old and New Testament).

Let's begin with God Himself and ask the simple question, "What does the Scripture reveal about God"? From the first book in the Bible, Genesis, it is clear that God is the Creator and Sustainer of the universe, and all that exists. As recorded in the Gospel of Matthew, 11:25, Jesus begins his prayer, "*O Father, Lord of heaven and earth . . .*" From the beginning to the end, the Scripture is consistent in describing God in that manner. Jesus, however, was unique in giving the Eternal God an unheard-of name to the religious people of his day, i.e. the Jews. Jesus sometimes referred to God as *Abba* which was one of the words used by young children for their father. In English, it can be rendered as, "*Daddy*". Such intimate terminology about the Eternal God was incomprehensible to the religious people of his day, e.g., the Jews in particular.

In Exodus 20:1-17, we find the *Ten Commandments.* Notice these are not presented as "*suggestions for successful living*", but rather as non-negotiable *rules* which are like *guard rails* for living. God's way as presented in these verses is the smart way to live. You are free to stray, so to speak, but there will be a price to pay. Ultimately you do not "*break*" the Ten Commandments, they "*break*" you. The Eternal God proclaims throughout the Old Testament that there is a right and a wrong way to live and that the categories of *good* and *evil* do exist.

It is hard to do better than the Creeds of antiquity, the Nicene and the Apostles Creeds. It would be a worthwhile endeavor to combine and analyze them to evaluate and bolster your belief system. You'll find them in their entirety in the Introduction.

In reality, one's belief systems are of critical importance for daily living and this is true at all levels. For instance, let's say you know virtually nothing about snakes, but you *believe* they are inherently harmless. So one day you step outside your door and there lies this beautiful, multicolored snake with bright bands of red, yellow, and black. You pick up what you *believe* to be a *harmless* snake. Turns out that coral snakes are deadly poisonous. So your *belief* system about snakes, especially this particular snake, has betrayed you with potentially very serious consequences. The practical solution to this problem is simply more information that is rooted in truth, not speculation.

The underlying axiom for living is simple: incorrect belief systems not based upon truth are dangerous. You are free to believe and can choose to believe pretty much anything you want to about any subject, but what matters is whether or not your *beliefs* are consistent with the way things are, with the truth. When I was 49 years old I was diagnosed with early-onset, severe, progressive coronary artery disease. I write now as a seventy-seven-year-old man who has survived four interventions that included angioplasty and the placement of five stents. Over the past 27 years, I was free to *believe* that taking the proper meds, watching my diet, and doing regular exercise were irrelevant to my well-being. But had I not embraced, to a certain degree, a reasonably healthy lifestyle, it likely would not have ended well for me. I wouldn't be writing this book. During my last visit with him, my cardiologist told me quite frankly that twenty-seven years ago he did not believe I would be among the living at this point! I would be remiss, however, if I did not give due credit to my Father who has blessed my meager efforts and that of my doctors and protected me all these years. So, Gracias a Dios!

I am a lifelong gardener. When dealing with nature in general, there are always underlying realities. You either inform yourself and learn about them, or you will not be a successful gardener. Things like proper soil preparation, plant spacing, adequate sunshine, weed, and insect control, etc. are critical. To be a successful gardener you have to follow the rules. You are free to do otherwise, but you will not likely have very many vegetables to enjoy and will have wasted lots of time and effort in the process. The principle is the same in all areas of life.

Jesus said, *"You have heard that it was said to the men of old . . . but I say to you . . . "* (Matthew 5:21, 22 RSV). In his *Sermon on the Mount*, Jesus spends most of the time debunking commonly held beliefs and behaviors that were opposed to His way as the *Revealer* of God's truth. So for the three years, He spent with the Twelve, Jesus encouraged and demanded that they move away from societal and religious norms, and belief systems, and adopt his ways of thinking about and doing life. And that also will be the nature of our journey with Him.

Atheism is the ultimate non-belief system. The vast majority of humankind over the eons of time and space are more prone to turn to false gods and idols, and thus commit idolatry. That is one way to be *dead* wrong. The Prophet Isaiah made fun of such folly:

> *"All those who make idols are worthless, and the gods they prize so highly are useless. Those who worship those gods are blind and ignorant – and they will be disgraced. It does no good to make a metal image to worship as a god! Everyone who worships it will be humiliated. The people who make idols are human beings and nothing more. Let them come and stand trial – they will be terrified and suffer disgrace.*
>
> *The metalworker takes a piece of metal and works with it over a fire. His strong arm swings a hammer to pound the metal into shape. As he works, he gets hungry, thirsty, and tired.*
>
> *The carpenter measures the wood. He outlines a figure with chalk, carves it out with tools, and makes it in the form of a man, a handsome human figure to be placed in his house. He might cut down cedars to use, or choose an oak or cypress wood from the forest. Or he might plant a laurel tree and wait for the rain to make it grow. A man uses part of a tree for fuel and part of it for making an idol. With one part he builds a fire to warm himself and bake bread; with the other part, he makes a god and worships it. With some of the wood he makes a fire, roasts meat, eats it, and is satisfied. He warms himself and says, "How nice and warm! What a beautiful fire!" The rest of the wood he makes into an idol, and then he bows down and worships it. He prays to it and says, "You are my god – save me!"*

Such people are too stupid to know what they are doing. They close their eyes and their minds to the truth. The maker of idols hasn't the wit or the sense to say, "Some of the wood I burned up. I baked some bread on coals, and I roasted meat and ate it. And the rest of the wood I made into an idol. Here I am bowing down to a block of wood!'

It makes as much sense as eating ashes. His foolish ideas have so misled him that he is beyond help.   He won't admit to himself that the idol he holds in his hand is not a god at all." (Isaiah 44:9-20 TEV)

Modern-day idolatry may not look as foolish as that described by Isaiah in the latter half of the eighth century B.C., but it is no less insidious and no less foolish. It would be an interesting project to identify what forms of idolatry look like in your world today, and which ones you might find most tempting.

The secret to formulating a set of beliefs about God is to become a lifetime student of God's Word. In today's world, there is no shortage of help in that regard. However, I offer one suggestion, maybe even a warning: Spend more time reading and studying the Bible itself and less time reading what someone else thinks about the Bible. Let God be your Teacher.

CHAPTER FIVE

RELATIONSHIP WITH OTHER BELIEVERS

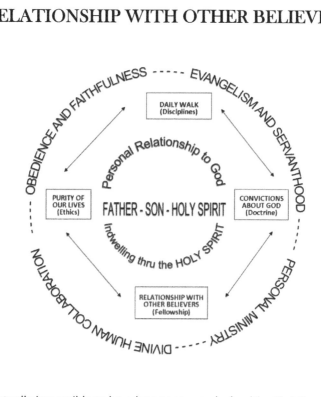

It is virtually impossible to be a *lone ranger* and a healthy Christian. You can survive as a lone Christian, but it is difficult to thrive. The Christian life thrives in the context of genuine fellowship with other believers. The Greek word translated as *fellowship* in the New Testament is *koinonia* (transliteration of the Greek). Dictionaries generally describe koinonia as *"intimate spiritual communion and participation in a common religious commitment and spiritual community."*[27] Koinonia appears 19 times in most editions of the New Testament, e.g., Acts 2:42.

Growing up in Del Rio, Texas, I attended the First Baptist Church with my family. I professed my faith in Jesus Christ and was baptized at ten years of age. Our family faithfully attended weekly church services and Sunday

---

[27] Merriam-Webster

School. That was pretty normal for a family at that time. I would describe those years and experiences at the same time as both uneventful and yet significant. I clearly remember taking my newfound faith and commitment to Christ seriously as a ten-year-old. I clearly remember one of my Sunday School teachers, a young man in pilot training at Laughlin Air Force Base. He impressed me as a serious Christian who genuinely cared about me and the others in that class.

I was twelve in the fall of 1957 when my family moved to Killeen in Central Texas. As a family, we joined the First Baptist Church and again, were regular attendees of worship and Sunday School. Several experiences stand out for me. John Shaeffer was a deacon and my Sunday School teacher and barber. He impressed me both as a man and as a Christian. When Mr. Schaeffer prayed, it seemed real and personal, like he was talking to Someone he knew. I thought that was rather unusual in that most public *church* prayers seemed to be scripted and did not sound like personal communication with the living God.

As a Senior in high school, I attended a Sunday night class called *Training Union* led by our pastor's wife, Mrs. Jean Harris. She took a special interest in me and encouraged me to seek out the Baptist Student Union at Texas A&M where I would attend in the Fall. That turned out to be a providential referral. I did get involved in BSU, served on the leadership team, was called to the ministry while at A&M, and after my seminary training became a Baptist Student Union Director, serving in that capacity for 25 years. However, it is my experience as a college student that is pertinent to our discussion here. As I began my life as a Christian college student I'm rather certain that I had never experienced genuine *koinonia* with other believers. That was a gift I had not received from God. As I said in Chapter One, it was during my junior year at A&M that I began meeting weekly with three or four fellow students with a hunger to know God and share our lives in Christ with a degree of honesty I had never experienced before. We studied Scripture, prayed together, and confessed our sins. It was powerful and my first experience of *koinonia*! That small group experience was transformational. To this day each of us is still engaged in serving the Lord.

Without a doubt, my life would not have taken the direction it did apart from that initial experience of genuine *koinonia* at Texas A&M. It was truly pivotal, and, in my career as a campus minister, I did my best to build an environment for college students which would provide opportunities for that level of fellowship.

At the very beginning of his public ministry, Jesus made a bold statement of his need to be a part of an intensive fellowship. In Mark 3:13,14 we read, *"And he went up into the hills, and called to him those whom he desired; and they came to him. And he appointed twelve to be with him . . ."*. (RSV) It is reasonable to assume that these men would have experienced *koinonia* during their three years of sharing life and ministry with Jesus. Yet, none of the four Gospel writers use that term to describe the disciple band. What we know is that they were a smorgasbord of personalities, temperaments, and backgrounds. Apart from the two sets of brothers, James and John, the sons of Zebedee, and Simon Peter and Andrew, the sons of Jonas, the disciples as a group were not friends before their association with Jesus.

At times Jesus scolded them and confronted their preconceptions as to his identity. They often exhibited a competitive spirit, musing as to who was Jesus' favorite, who would sit at his *right hand* in the Kingdom. They misunderstood Jesus' teaching about servanthood, and true greatness as being the *"servant of all"* (Mark 9:35 RSV). It seems Jesus' focus was on teaching them and demonstrating to them the true nature of the Kingdom of God and himself as the Son of God. His priorities were not their priorities; his perspective, not theirs. That was evident on numerous occasions such as His conversation with the woman at the well, and the feeding of the five thousand. As those initial months and then years went by, we can assume that their fellowship deepened, and matured alongside their ever-increasing understanding of the person and message of Jesus. At the very heart of his message was this command which he gave to his close friends, the Twelve:

> *"A new commandment I give to you, that you love one another; even as I have loved you, that you also love one another. 35 By this all men will know that you are my disciples, if you have love for one another."* John 13:34, 35 (RSV)

41

Concerning the ministry of Jesus, Elton Trueblood writes, *"All he did was to collect a few uncompromising men, inspire them with the sense of his vocation and theirs, and build their lives into an **intensive fellowship** of affection, worship, and work."*[28]

From Dr. Luke's writings in The Gospel of Luke and the book of Acts, you might surmise that experiencing *koinonia* is a post-Crucifixion/Resurrection/Ascension/Pentecost phenomenon. Since, as we understand it, and as described in Acts, the church was born during those tumulous times. (re: Acts, Chapters 1 & 2) It is in Acts 2:42 that Dr. Luke uses the Greek, *koinonia* (translated as *fellowship*), for the first time in the New Testament to describe in part the nature of the common life of these early Christians who would become the Church, the Body of Christ on earth. The remainder of the Book of Acts centers around those early groups of believers gathered in *house churches* scattered over the world of New Testament times, experiencing genuine *koinonia*.

> *"And they devoted themselves to the apostles' teaching and* ***fellowship***, *to the breaking of bread and the prayers."* (Acts 2:42) RSV)

From that point forward the New Testament, letters to churches, pastors, etc., focus on their life together, their *fellowship*. Why? Because only when fellowship is real and authentic can the Lord do his very best work in his world. The reality is that genuine fellowship *". . . is something which we cannot produce at will, but we do have the modest function of meeting some of the conditions of its emergence."*[29] That becomes the responsibility of every believer to some degree and in various circumstances.

Each of Paul's letters addressed specific issues in the various churches related to the quality of their life together and their fellowship. Five of the sixteen chapters of Romans (30%), chapters 12-16, deal with the nature of

---

[28] Trueblood, Elton. Alternative to Futility. (New York: Harper and Row), 1949.
[29] Trueblood, Elton. The Incendiary Fellowship. (New York: Harper and Row), 1967, p. 55.

their fellowship, personal responsibility for such, functions within the Body of Christ, the supremacy of love as the glue that keeps the fellowship intact, impediments to genuine fellowship such as judging others, self-interest, etc. In the final chapter, Romans 16:1-16 consists of Paul's listing of thirty-plus individuals/friends to whom he sends personal greetings, thus underlining the simple fact that genuine fellowship in Christ, *koinonia*, is all about relationships and friendships. In the final few verses, he issues this warning: *"I urge you, my brothers: Watch out for those who cause divisions and upset people's faith . . ."* (Romans 16:17 TEV)

To **the church in Corinth** Paul focuses on a similar theme, unity. I Corinthians 1:10 - *"I appeal to you, brothers, by the authority of our Lord Jesus Christ: agree, all of you, in what you say, so there will be no divisions among you; be completely united, with only one thought and one purpose."* (TEV) Chapters five and six address the issue of sexual immorality which is not to be tolerated in the church, the Body of Christ. I Corinthians 6:19, 20 sums up Paul's appeal, *"Don't you know that your body is the temple of the Holy Spirit, who lives in you, the Spirit given you by God? You do not belong to yourselves but to God; He bought you for a price. So use your bodies for God's glory."* (TEV) I Corinthians, Chapter 13, is fondly referred to as the *love* chapter. As such, all or part of it is traditionally read as part of marriage ceremonies. It is important to understand that the lofty admonitions in that chapter were intended for the Body of Christ in Corinth, not just married couples!

In Today's English Version of the New Testament, Paul's letter to **the church at Ephesus**, Chapter four is titled, *The Unity of the Body*, and in verses 3-6, Paul says, *"Do your best to preserve the unity which the Spirit gives, by the peace that binds you together. There is one body and one Spirit, just as there is one hope to which God has called you. There is one Lord, one faith, one baptism; there is one God and Father of all men, who is Lord of all, works through all, and is in all."* (TEV) The title for Chapter five is "Living in the Light". Ephesians 5:1,2 says, *"Since you are God's dear children, you must try to be like Him. Your life must be controlled by love, just as Christ loved us and gave his life for us, as a sweet-smelling offering and sacrifice which pleases God."* (TEV)

In Paul's letter to the Philippians, he continues the same theme of unity as crucial to koinonia, genuine fellowship in the church. Philippians 2:2 – *"I urge you then, make me completely happy by having the same thoughts, sharing the same love, and being one in soul and mind."* (TEV)

It's not Paul's last letter, but this cursory summary of Paul's writings needs to come to an end with a few verses from Paul's letter to the church at Colossae! Colossians 3:12-17 – *"You are the people of God: he loved you and chose you for his own. Therefore, you must put on compassion, kindness, humility, gentleness, and patience. Be helpful to one another, and forgive one another, whenever any of you has a complaint against someone else. You must forgive each other in the same way that the Lord has forgiven you. And to all these add love, which binds all things together in perfect unity. The peace that Christ gives is to be the judge in your hearts; for to this peace, God has called you together in the one body. And be thankful. Christ's message, in all its richness, must live in your hearts. Teach and instruct each other with all wisdom. Sing psalms, hymns, and sacred songs; sing to God, with thanksgiving in your hearts. Everything you do or say, then, should be done in the name of the Lord Jesus, as you give thanks through him to God the Father."* (TEV)

The Gospel of John, Chapters 13-17, records in great detail the final night of Jesus' betrayal, and before that, his time with the Twelve in the Upper Room. Chapter 17 records, what is often termed, Jesus' "Priestly Prayer", for the Twelve. In that prayer, Jesus reveals his conviction regarding the absolute significance of unity in their fellowship. Following is a list of Jesus's requests to the Father: *"... that they may be one just as You and I are one."* (vs. 11),

"I pray that they may all be one. Father! May they be in us, just as you are in me and I am in you. May they be one, so that the world will believe that you sent me." (vs. 21), *"I gave them the same glory you gave me, so that they may be one, just as you and I are one."* (vs. 22), *"I in them and you in me, so that they may be completely one, in order that the world may know that you sent me and that you love them as you love me."* (TEV) Could Jesus have possibly made himself clearer in this prayer for the Twelve?

AUTHENTIC CHRISTIAN FELLOWSHIP IS . . .

. . . a fellowship of deeply committed followers of Jesus Christ, with their lives centered around God the Father, Son, and Holy Spirit.
. . . made up of real people, who are honest and transparent, and who are learning to *"speak the truth in love"* in their life together with fellow believers.
. . . a fellowship characterized by joy (John 5), unity (John 17), and love (John 13:34,35).
. . . a fellowship in which lives are constantly being changed by the Presence of the Risen Christ.

CONCLUSION FINAL WORD

Hopefully, I have made the point that experiencing *koinonia* is crucial, desirable, and unpredictable. It is a gift of God given in the context of a small group of earnest Christians by God's Holy Spirit.

So what can you do as an individual since you cannot *make it happen*? You can ask the Good Lord to lead you to a church or fellowship of believers with a spiritual environment conducive to *koinonia*, i.e. one that includes and considers small group fellowships as integral to their scheme of ministry. In your present church affiliation, you might also assume the role of encourager and instigator of a small group in which koinonia just might have a chance to happen!

CHAPTER SIX

PURITY OF OUR LIVES

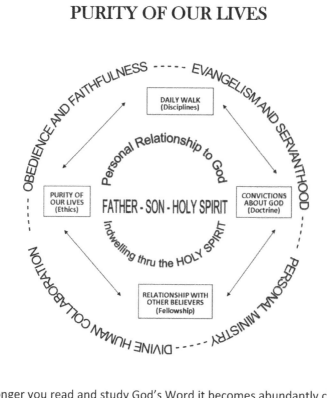

The longer you read and study God's Word it becomes abundantly clear that personal purity, morality, and ethical behavior are a big deal to God. You simply cannot please Him and live in a manner contrary to His revealed truths about what is moral/immoral, pure/impure, right/wrong. In the first few chapters of Genesis, that point is clear. It is stunning to think that the very first act of immorality and impurity was nothing less than Cain's murdering his brother, Abel. And he paid a heavy price for that evil deed. (Genesis 4:1-16). In the Good News Bible (TEV), Chapter Six of Genesis is subtitled, "The Wickedness of Mankind", and what follows is the story of Noah, his family, and the great flood. *"This is the story of Noah. He had three sons, Shem, Ham, and Japheth. Noah had no faults and was the only good man of his time. He lived in fellowship with God, but everyone else was evil in God's sight, and violence had spread everywhere. God said to Noah, 'I have decided to put an end to all mankind. I will destroy them completely because the world is full of their*

violent deeds.'" In light of this ancient story, to say that God is serious about evil, impurity, and immorality, is somewhat of an understatement!

Following God's rescuing His people from slavery in Egypt, and years of wandering around in the desert with Moses leading them, on Mt. Sinai Moses received the Ten Commandments (Exodus 19). They provide an excellent summary of what God expects from those who choose to follow Him. They were literally written in stone, and therefore provide no option for revision! They stand as relevant today as they were when originally given to the people of God in the wilderness of Mt Sinai.

As you continue reading in the Old Testament, the recurring theme is infidelity to God (idolatry) and immoral behavior (impurity) on the part of God's people and their leaders, various kings over the centuries. A few pleased God, but most did not. There were only a few exceptions. The price paid for their idolatry and immorality was high, ending in the fall of Jerusalem to the Babylonians (586 B.C.), the destruction of the Temple, and the people of Judah being taken in exile to Babylonia. It was a sad fate indeed *for God's people*, the heavy price of infidelity and impurity.

Proverbs is a collection of moral and religious teachings with no apparent thematic arrangement. In addition to various admonitions regarding life in general, e.g., the folly of laziness gets a lot of attention! There is a recurring theme of the danger of an impure and immoral lifestyle. Contrasted over and over is righteous vs wicked behavior, the two being compared in terms of positive and negative outcomes. The point is made in various ways, but the bottom line: it is never *wise* to *break the rules* of human decency, morality, and purity.

Over the centuries from Isaiah to Malachi the Old Testament Prophets, in both word and action, pleaded with God's people to renew their faithfulness to God and repent of their wickedness, rebellion, and sin. The prophetic word was a word of warning to God's people of the inevitable results of disobedience and immorality which would bring doom and destruction upon the nation. Each of the seventeen prophetic books had a unique setting in terms of time and circumstance, but their general theme was consistently the same: God's people are called to live in fidelity to God, to be righteous and pure in thought and deed.

THE FOUR GOSPELS

The Four Gospels, Matthew, Mark, Luke, and John, record the life, public ministry, and teaching of Jesus which began when he was about 30 years old. The first three Gospels are referred to as the *Synoptic Gospels* in that they give accounts of Jesus from the same point of view. Each of them is chronological and progressive from Jesus' birth to death, but in telling the story, they are also very different in style and even content, with Mark being the shortest. Matthew is written more from a Jewish perspective, and Luke to the Gentile followers of Christ of his time. The Gospel of John is noticeably different in style, content, and focus. John's Gospel is theological, interpretive, and less inclined to follow a strict timeline. In John, you find several *stories* about Jesus not recorded in the Synoptic Gospels. Each of the four Gospels is fascinating to read and study and you have the rest of your life to enjoy that adventure! In keeping with the focus of this chapter, I want to single out a few passages in each of the four Gospels that speak to the theme of this chapter, the "Purity of Our Lives".

In the Gospel of Matthew, Chapters 5-7, you'll find the fullest account of Jesus' Sermon on the Mount, which begins with *The Beatitudes*. Matthew 5:6,8 say, *"Blessed are those who hunger and thirst for righteousness, for they shall be satisfied . . . Blessed are the pure in heart, for they shall see God."* (RSV) Matthew 5:43,44, 45, 48, *"You have heard it that it was said, 'You shall love your neighbor and hate your enemy.' But I say to you, Love your enemies and pray for those who persecute you, so that you may be sons of your Father who is in heaven . . ."* The paragraph concludes with, *"You, therefore, must be perfect, as your heavenly Father is perfect."* (RSV)

Mark 7:1-23 records an interesting encounter between Jesus and some Pharisees and teachers of the Jewish Law. They came to Jesus with a complaint regarding his disciples and their failure to properly *clean their hands* before eating. For the Jewish hierarchy, purity, ethics, and morality were all about following manmade guidelines. Don't get the wrong idea. This discussion was not about sanitation, but rather about the meticulous and endless *rules* for daily living including ritually cleaning your hands before eating. There were many other rules including the proper way to wash cups, pots, copper bowls, and beds. Jesus challenged them, quoting the Prophet Isaiah, *"These people, says God, honor me with their words, but their heart is really far away from me…"* (Isaiah 29:13 TEV) In speaking to the crowd of ordinary folks who were enjoying the back and forth between Jesus and the Jewish leaders, He said this: *"There is nothing that goes into a person from the outside which can make him ritually unclean. Rather, it is what comes out of a person that him unclean."* (Mark 7:14, 15, TEV) Finally, he left the crowd and went into a house with his disciples. He reiterated what he had said to the people and then added: *"For from the inside, from a person's heart, come the evil ideas which lead him to do immoral things, to rob, kill, commit adultery, be greedy, and do all sorts of evil things; deceit, indecency, jealousy, slander, pride, and folly – all these evil things come from inside a person and make him unclean."* (Mark 7:21-23 TEV)

Hypocrisy is defined as *". . . pretending to be what one is not, pretended sanctity, a pretense of virtue, piety, etc."*[30] That was the main accusation Jesus made against the Jewish hierarchy of his day, the Pharisees. *" As thousands of people crowded together so that they were stepping on each other, Jesus said first to his disciples, 'Be on guard against the yeast of the Pharisees – I mean their hypocrisy. Whatever is covered up will be uncovered, and every secret will be made known. So then, whatever you have said in the dark will be heard in broad daylight, and whatever you have whispered in private in a closed room will be shouted from the housetops."* (Luke 12:1-3 TEV) Even after a couple of thousand years, these words of Jesus are sobering indeed. It lifts our discussion of the *purity of our lives* to a different level. In Jesus' parable of the rich fool, he focuses on a particular version of purity/impurity – greed. *"A man in the crowd said to Jesus, 'Teacher, tell my brother to divide with me the property our father left us. Jesus answered him, 'Man, who gave me the right to judge or divide the property between you two?' And he went on to say to them all, ' Watch out and guard yourselves from every kind of greed; because a person's true life is not made up of the things he owns, no matter how rich he may be.'"* Then Jesus told a brief story about a rich man who was blessed with a bumper crop on his farmland, so much in abundance, it would not fit in his barns. So he decided to tear them down

---

[30] Websters New World Dictionary

and build bigger barns to hold his bumper crop. He was very pleased with himself and very happy with the prospects of enjoying his bounty. Jesus concluded the parable in this way, *"But God said to him, 'You fool! This very night you will have to give up your life; then who will get all these things you have kept for yourself?' And Jesus concluded, " This is how it is with those who pile up riches for themselves but are not rich in God's sight."* (Luke 12:13-21 TEV)

The Gospel of John, as previously mentioned is different from the Synoptic Gospels. You'll not find the *Sermon on the Mount* or most of the other prominent features of the other three. That is also true in what John does not say about *purity* per se. Two passages that relate to sexual purity are included: John 4:1-30, titled *"Jesus and the Samaritan Woman"* in the TEV, presents Jesus as not judging her behavior in the arena of sex and marriage but revealing himself to her as Messiah. Although this woman had multiple men she was sleeping with or had been married to, He did not explicitly condemn her behavior, but He did love her, accept her, and in the process changed her life forever. It was a lengthy encounter and was still in progress when his disciples returned from a trip to town to get some food. John 4:27 says it this way, *"At that moment Jesus' disciples returned, and they were greatly surprised to find him talking with a woman. But none of them said to her, "What do you want?' or asked him, 'Why are you talking with her?"* In the meantime, the woman headed back home and said to the people there, *"Come and see the man who told me everything I have ever done. Could he be the Messiah?"* So they left the town and went to Jesus."* (John 4:29,30 TEV)

The second passage recorded by John that has a connection to *purity* is John 8:1-11, titled. *"The Woman Caught in Adultery,"* in the TEV. His approach was virtually the same with this woman who was brought to him for judgment. He ended up condemning her accusers as hypocrites and changing her life as well, with the question and admonition, *"Where are they? Is there no one left to condemn you? 'No one sir', she answered. 'Well, then, Jesus said. 'I do not condemn you either. Go, but do not sin again.' "*

ACTS TO THE REVELATION

The remainder of the New Testament, from Acts to Revelation, is a rich resource of material on the subject of the purity of our lives as followers of Christ. All twenty-three of these New Testament books/letters contain material in one way or another that underlines the absolute necessity of moral and ethical purity in the churches and the individuals in those churches. Virtually all the problems addressed in those books/letters were rooted in some kind of ethical breach of the accepted standards of the Christian community. It is not within the purview of this book to review each remaining book/letter with *purity* in mind, so I will *cherry-pick* a selection of passages that are representative of the whole.

The Acts of the Apostles, written by Dr. Luke in AD 62 or 63, was in effect a history of the young church. Acts 2:43-45 is an interesting look into the communal life among the believers: *"Many miracles and wonders were being done through the apostles, and everyone was filled with awe. All the believers continued together in close fellowship and shared their belongings with one another. They would sell their property and possessions, and distribute the money among all, according to what each one needed."* (TEV) It seems this particular arrangement was a one-time happening as we have no mention of such in the remainder of the New Testament. Acts 5:1-11 is about two members of that early group of believers, Ananias and his wife, Sapphira. As the story is told, they, too, sold some property but together agreed to keep part of the money and turn the remainder over to the apostles. In verse three, *"Peter says to him, 'Ananias, why did you let Satan take control of you and make you lie to the Holy Spirit by keeping part of the money you received for the property?'"... Why did you decide to do such a thing? You have not lied to men – you have lied to God!' As soon as Ananias heard this, he fell down dead; ...".* (TEV)

The story continues in verses 7-10, *"About three hours later his wife, not knowing what had happened, came in. Peter asked her, 'Tell me, was this the full amount you and your husband received for your property? 'Yes', she answered, 'the full amount.' So Peter said to her, 'Why did you and your husband decide to put the Lord's Spirit to the test? The men who buried your husband are at the door right now, and they will carry you out too!' At once she fell down at his feet and died."* (TEV) Lying was not a capital offense and most certainly God did not strike them dead on the spot. Having been caught and confronted by Peter in their misrepresentation, their lie, the shock of it all likely precipitated cardiac arrest! The point here is plain; deceit/lying was a form of impurity unacceptable within this early fellowship of believers. Their sin was not keeping part of the money, just lying about it!

The first chapter of the Apostle Paul's letter to the Romans has a section titled, "The Guilt of Mankind". It is a vivid, gruesome, and detailed description of immorality that is the polar opposite of purity. It serves no purpose in this setting to enumerate those sinful behaviors. This immorality is attributed to the ungodly, to persons who do not acknowledge God and do not consider his *laws* of morality relevant. The world of the first century was not exactly a welcoming environment for followers of Christ! Romans 12:2 implores readers, *"Do not conform yourselves to the standards of this world, but let God transform you inwardly by a complete change of your mind. Then you will be able to know the will of God – what is good and is pleasing to him and is perfect".* (TEV)

In Galatians 5:19-26, Paul paints a vivid contrast between *"What human nature does . . .",* and the kind of fruit God's Holy Spirit produces in one's life – *" . . . love, joy, peace, patience, kindness, goodness, faithfulness, humility, and self-control . . .".* Paul concludes, *"And those who belong to Christ Jesus have put to death their human nature with all its passions and desires. The Spirit has given us life, he must also control our lives."* (TEV)

Paul continues in his letter to the Ephesians with pleas to his readers like these: *"I urge you, then – I am a prisoner because I serve the Lord: live a life that **measures up to the standard God set** when he called you. Be always humble, gentle, and patient . . . ".* *"In the Lord's name, then, I warn you: **do not continue to live like the heathen**, whose thoughts are worthless and whose minds are in the dark. They have no part in the life that God gives, for they are completely ignorant and stubborn."* (Ephesians 4:1,2 TEV) And then in 5:1,2, *"Since you are God's dear children, you must **try to be like him**. Your life must be controlled by love . . .".* (TEV)

Paul continues with passionate admonitions to righteousness in Philippians, Colossians, I Thessalonians, and Titus: *"Do everything without complaining or arguing, so that you may be **innocent and pure as God's perfect children**, who live in a world of corrupt and sinful people. You must shine among them like stars lighting up the sky, as you offer them the message of life."* (Philippians 2:14-16 TEV) *"You must **put to death, then, the earthly desires at work in you**, such as sexual immorality, indecency, lust, evil passions, and greed (for greed is a form of idolatry)."* *"**You are the people of God**; he loved you and chose you for his own. So then, **you must clothe yourselves** with compassion, kindness, humility, gentleness, and patience. Be tolerant with one another and forgive one another . . ."* (Colossians 3:5,12,13 TEV) Paul describes to the Thessalonians "A Life That Pleases God" with these words: *"Finally, our brothers, you learned from us how you should live in order to please God. . . God wants you to be holy and completely free from sexual immorality. . . God did not call us to live in immorality, but in holiness."* (I Thessalonians 4:1-7 TEV) Paul's letter to Titus is addressed to his young helper/pastor including guidelines for church leaders and members. Paul urges Titus to teach the church *sound doctrine* that included these instructions about purity: *"For God has revealed his grace for the salvation of all mankind. That grace instructs us to give up ungodly living and worldly passions, and to live self-controlled, upright, and godly lives in this world . . ."* (Titus 2:11,12 TEV)

Under the heading, "Instructions and Warnings" in the TEV, the author of Hebrews says, *"Try to be at peace with everyone, and try to live a holy life because no one will see the Lord without it."* (Hebrews 12:14 TEV) *Appearances* matter and there is a direct link between the purity of our lives and our effectiveness in sharing the Gospel with folks within our sphere of influence.

The Book of James is not written to an individual or a church in particular. James says this letter is addressed to *". . . all God's people scattered over the whole world."* (James 1:1 TEV) James suggests that both subtraction and addition are keys to *purity: "Remember this, my dear brothers! Everyone must be slow to speak and slow to become angry. Man's anger does not achieve God's righteous purpose. So get rid of every filthy habit and all wicked conduct . . ."* (James 1:19-21 TEV) *"Is there anyone among you who is wise and understanding? He is to prove it by his good life, by his good deeds performed with humility and wisdom. . . . Where there is jealousy and selfishness, there is also disorder and every kind of evil. But the wisdom from above is pure first of all; it is also peaceful, gentle, and friendly; it is full of compassion and produces a harvest of good deeds; it is free from prejudice and hypocrisy. And goodness is the harvest that is produced from the seeds the peacemakers plant in peace."* (James 3:13-18 TEV)

We conclude our cursory survey of the New Testament with the writings of Peter and John, two of Jesus' best friends. If anyone knew the heart of Jesus on this matter it would be these two. We begin with Peter. I Peter was written to encourage Christians who were scattered all over the northern part of Asia Minor and were facing severe persecution. (I Peter 1:1 TEV) In that setting, Peter encouraged them, saying, *"Be obedient to God and do not allow your lives to be shaped by those desires you had when you were still ignorant. Instead, be holy in all that you do, just as God who called you is holy. The Scripture says, "Be holy because I am holy.'"* (I Peter 1:14-16 (TEV) He continues in Chapter 2, *"I appeal to you my friends, as strangers and refugees in this world! Do not give in to bodily passions, which are always at war against the soul. Your conduct among the heathen should be so good that when they accuse you of being evildoers, they will have to recognize your good deeds and so praise God on the Day of his coming."* (I Peter 2:11,12 TEV) Peter begins chapter four reminding these Christians of their changed lives. *"From now on then, you must live the rest of your earthly lives controlled by God's will and not by human desires. You have spent enough time in the past doing what the heathen do."* (I Peter 4:2,3 TEV)

John wrote his first letter to help his readers understand what it means to live in fellowship with the Living God - Father, Son, and Holy Spirit. He begins like this: *"Now the message that we have heard from his Son and announce is this: God is light, and there is no darkness at all in him. If then, we say that we have fellowship with him, yet at the same time live in the darkness, we are lying both in our words and in our actions. But if we live in the light – just as he is in the light – then we have fellowship with one another, and the blood of Jesus, his Son, purifies us from every sin."* (I John 1:5-7 TEV) The words used in this passage, *light and darkness*, are just another way of saying *purity and impurity*.

John continues in chapter two with these words, *"Do not love the world or anything that belongs to the world. If you love the world, you do not love the Father. Everything that belongs to the world – what the sinful self desires, what people see and want, and everything in this world that people are so proud of – none of this comes from the Father; it all comes from the world. The world and everything in it that people desire is passing away, but he who does the will of God lives forever."* (I John 2:15-17 TEV) John speaks in absolutes, and that's why his words and message are so powerful. He does not dance around the truth. There's no way to misunderstand the point he is making. The first paragraph of chapter three is one of my favorites in all of the New Testament. *"My dear friends, we are now God's children, but it is not yet clear what we shall become. But we know that when Christ appears, we shall be like him because we shall see him as he is. **Everyone who has this hope in Christ keeps himself pure, just as Christ is pure.**"* (I John 3;2,3 TEV) Like I said previously, you just cannot get any clearer than the Word of God!

We conclude our New Testament *word study* on purity with *"The Revelation to John"* as titled in Today's English Version. Chapter three, *"The Message to Sardis"*, deserves our attention. *"To the angel of the church in Sardis write: 'I know that you have the reputation of being alive, even though you are dead! So wake up, and strengthen what you still have before it dies completely. For I find that what you have done is **not yet perfect** in the sight of my God. Remember, then, what you were taught and what you heard; obey it and **turn from your sins** . . . but **a few of you** there in Sardis have **kept your clothes clean**. You will walk with me, **clothed in white** because you are worthy to do so.'"* (Revelation 3:1-5 TEV) In terms of the *purity of our lives*, it seems our goal as followers of Jesus Christ would be to be among the *few* deemed worthy to be *"clothed in white"* and invited to *"walk with Him"* in Glory!

I find myself wanting to *apologize* about how much Scripture I have quoted in this chapter. What I have discovered is that what I want to say about purity cannot be said any better than the words of Scripture. That is especially true in that, for the most part, I'm using Today's English Version, which reads like your daily newspaper, and needs very little interpretation.

21st CENTURY ETHICAL CHALLENGES FOR CHRISTIANS

It could be argued that the two most pressing ethical issues facing God's people today are the *sanctity of life/abortion* and *sexuality/gender*. Both represent enormous and extremely complicated subjects that are impossible to adequately deal with in the context of this book and this chapter on purity in particular. I have recently read six books on the subject of sexuality from both a Christian and non-Christian perspective. The reading was helpful but not conclusive and I find myself back to the place I started from. There are *answers* to the ethical dilemmas facing us today, but they are far from *black and white* for a thoughtful person. The Bible is certainly not silent in these matters and I will offer several references for your perusal. The simple fact that sincere Christians and bonafide churches and denominations have arrived at opposite points of view illustrates the complexity of these ethical conundrums.

One of my former students and friend, Autumn Dawn Galbreath, MD, said it well in a recent dialogue with me: "*Sexual choices are, along with many other choices, a critical piece of spiritual health, vitality, and holiness and warrant a great deal of prayer, study, and discussion within the Christian community, rather than accepting the widespread message of our culture.*"[31]

The Scripture is quite clear in principle on matters of the sanctity of life and homosexuality. Yes, they are *clear*, and yet they are not *easy* to apply in real-life situations involving our network of family and friends. Here is a short list of readings from God's Word: Sanctity of life, Psalm 139:13-16. Sexuality, Genesis 1:26-28 and 2:22-24. Jesus, Matthew 19:4-6.

---

[31] Autumn Dawn Galbreath, MD, January 16, 2023

CONCLUSION

We have looked through the lens of the Holy Scripture at the topic, *"The Purity of Our Lives"*. From Genesis to Revelation, the message is consistent – it matters greatly to God how we behave in this life. Various words and metaphors are used throughout to make the singular point that goes back to Leviticus 11:44, *"I am the Lord your God, and you must keep yourself holy, because I am holy."* (TEV)

CHAPTER SEVEN

OBEDIENCE AND FAITHFULNESS

Sometimes it is helpful to look at the synonyms and antonyms of keywords side by side to fully understand the concept. The Merriam-Webster Thesaurus lists these words as synonyms and antonyms of obedience: *"compliance, conformity, submission, and subordination"*, and then, *"disobedience, defiance, insubordination, rebelling, self-will, disrespect"*. The Thesaurus lists these words for faithfulness: *"allegiance, commitment, dedication, fidelity, loyalty, piety, reliability"*, and to the contrary, *"unfaithfulness, disloyalty, infidelity, falsity, treachery"*.

Obedience and faithfulness are related but they are not the same. Obedience is *cut and dried*, clear cut, yes or no. There is no middle ground; it has to do with complying with an order from someone who is your superior, as in the military, or in sports where your coach is in charge. Faithfulness has more to do with a relationship – commitment to a person or a cause, fidelity. More specifically, fidelity despite hardship, persecution, or temptation, perhaps marriage is the best example. Marriage does not work long-term apart from faithfulness.

Perhaps one of the most obvious arenas for observing *obedience and faithfulness* in real-time is with pets, dogs in particular, but horses also fit the paradigm. A well-trained dog or horse is a marvel to behold. With that kind of animal, all sorts of things for the good are possible. On the contrary, an untrained, disobedient dog is a pain to be around, because the dog's owner is not in charge of the animal. We have all been in those situations. An untrained horse is simply dangerous. Dogs are universally praised for their faithfulness to their master, even unto death.

In the context of family, the relationship between parents and children covers the gamut of the obedient/disobedient spectrum. It is sad indeed to be around a Mom or Dad who is not respected by or obeyed by their children.

If you refer to a Biblical concordance for these two words or versions thereof, you'll be amazed at the extent to which they are used in the Old and New Testaments. For example, the Concordance in the Revised Standard Version lists 53 references for *obedience* and 56 for *faithfulness*. So for this chapter, we will need to be very selective. It is important to keep in mind that obedience/faithfulness should be seen in the proper context and that context is one's relationship with God. The *Discipleship Model* hopefully makes that clear.

OLD TESTAMENT PASSAGES

The whole of Scripture, Old, and New Testaments, demonstrates that obedience/faithfulness is both individual and corporate in the eyes of God. A person's well-being and ultimate destiny are directly related to both. Over and over we read in the Old Testament of either the blessing and prosperity or judgment and demise of God's people based upon their failure to be obedient and faithful to Him. King Uzziah and his Son, Jotham, of Judah are perfect examples.

> *"Uzziah became king at the age of sixteen, and he ruled in Jerusalem for fifty-two years. Following the example of his father, he did what was pleasing to the Lord. As long as Zechariah, his religious advisor, was living, he served the Lord faithfully, and God blessed him. . . . His fame spread everywhere, and he became very powerful because of the help he received from God.* **But**

when King Uzziah became strong, he grew arrogant, and that led to his downfall. He defied (disobeyed) the Lord his God by going into the Temple to burn incense on the altar of incense. (He was sternly warned by the priests that it was not his place to do so and that he had disobeyed God with his foolish actions.) Azariah, the high priest said to him, *'Leave this holy place. You have offended the Lord God, and you no longer have his blessing.' Uzziah was standing there in the Temple beside the incense altar and was holding an incense burner. He became angry with the priests, and immediately a dreaded skin disease broke out on his forehead. For the rest of his life, King Uzziah was ritually unclean because of his disease. Unable to enter the Temple again, he lived in his own house, relieved of all duties, while his son Jotham governed the country."* II Chronicles 26:1-21 TEV

King Uzziah's son became king at the age of twenty-five and ruled Judah for sixteen years. The Scripture says, *"He did what was pleasing to the Lord, just as his father had done, but unlike his father, he did not sin by burning incense in the Temple."* The final assessment of Jotham's rule as King of Judah as recorded in II Chronicles 27:6 TEV is noteworthy: *"Jotham grew powerful because he **faithfully obeyed** the Lord his God."*

The above storyline is repeated over and over in I and II Chronicles, and elsewhere in the Old Testament. Obedience and faithfulness lead to success and blessing. Disobedience and unfaithfulness lead to failure and judgment. The corporate aspect of obedience and faithfulness is well illustrated in this passage in II Chronicles 24:18, 19 – *"And so the people stopped worshipping in the Temple of the Lord, the God of their ancestors, and began to worship idols and the images of the goddess Asherah. Their guilt for these sins brought the Lord's anger on Judah and Jerusalem. The Lord sent prophets to warn them to return to him but the people refused to listen."* (TEV) The ultimate end of King Joash and the people of Judah is recorded in II Chronicles 24:23-24: *"When autumn came that year, the Syrian army attacked Judah and Jerusalem, killed all the leaders, and took large amounts of loot back to Damascus. The Syrian army was small, but the Lord let them defeat a much larger Judean army because the people had abandoned him, the Lord God of their ancestors".* (TEV)

As I continue writing this chapter, I find myself in somewhat of a quandary on two fronts. In the first place, the themes of *obedience and faithfulness* are embedded in the Scripture to the degree that almost every page, chapter, and book, in the Old and New Testaments either explicitly or implicitly contains material related to one or the other. They are like Siamese twins. Secondly, with the understanding that I will likely be misunderstood, I confess to you that obedience and faithfulness have been more or less *natural* for me from the get-go. In essence, I am a boring, single-minded guy. I've had only one cell phone number for 40 years; I've had the same lovely wife for 55 years; I had only one career, campus ministry, for forty-one years; my passions are unchanged – my marriage and family, hunting, fishing, carpentry, gardening, and writing. I started an early morning quiet time that included daily journal entries when I was a student at A&M, 1963-1967, and have been faithful to such with only a few lapses over the years. At present, I have accumulated 3,800+ pages in my journal. Beginning in my forties, because of being diagnosed with early-onset, aggressive coronary heart disease, I took up the discipline of walking a couple of miles each day. Being *faithful* to that discipline is likely one of the reasons I am alive to this day according to my cardiologist of 27 years, Dr. Charles Roeth. So you get the point. I tend to be an *obedient and faithful* person in the various dimensions of my life, due partly to my inherent nature, but also rooted in my understanding of the crucial importance of those traits to a successful life as a follower of Jesus Christ. Again, I beg your pardon for my self-adulation. Truth be known, I reckon I have had my lapses over the years and may have conveniently chosen to forget them. Our Father, the Good Lord, is our ultimate Judge in such matters!

Regarding the message of Scripture on the subject of obedience and faithfulness, I will simply *cherry-pick* a few more key Old Testament passages, and then focus attention on the New Testament. In I Samuel we read about Eli, the Lord's priest at the time, and his sons (also Priests) who were described as scoundrels "... *who paid no attention to the Lord or to the regulations concerning what the priests could demand from the people*". (I Samuel 2:12,13, TEV) The sacrificial system included provisions for the priests to be fed by taking part of the sacrifices to be burned on the altar for themselves With Eli's sons the system was perverted in such a way as to anger the Lord. His question to Eli summed up the problem: *"Why do you look with greed at the sacrifices and offerings which I require from my people? Why, Eli, do you honor your sons more than me by letting them **fatten themselves** on the best parts of all the sacrifices my people offer to me?"* (I Samuel 2:29 TEV) God's judgment was severe: *"No one in your family will ever again live to old age. . . . When your two sons Hophni and Phinehas both die on the same day, this will show you that everything I have said will come true."* (I Samuel 2:32,33 TEV) Then comes the pronouncement about the person who would follow Eli and his sons. The Lord says, *"I will choose a priest **who will be faithful** to me and do everything I want him to."* (2:35) i.e., a priest who will be faithful and obedient! That person was Samuel who proved himself to be everything the Lord needed and wanted him to be.

The book of Nehemiah describes the events surrounding the rebuilding of the wall around Jerusalem. After the wall was completed Nehemiah chose two men to be in charge of Jerusalem and described them in this manner. *" I gave my brother Hanani and Hananiah, the governor of the castle (commanding officer of the fortress), charge over Jerusalem, for he was **a more faithful** and God-fearing man than many."* (Nehemiah 7:2 RSV) Throughout the book of Psalms, the Lord affirms those who are faithful to him, over and over. E.g. Psalms 18:25, *"O Lord, **you are faithful** to **those who are faithful** to you; completely good to those who are perfect."* (TEV) Psalms 50:5, *"Gather my **faithful** people to me . . .".* (TEV), and Psalms 101:6, *"I will look with favor on the **faithful** in the land that they may dwell with me: he who walks in the way that is blameless shall minister to me."* (RSV) Finally, Psalms 128:1-4, *"Happy are those **who obey the Lord, who live by his commands**. Your work will provide for your needs; you will be happy and prosperous. Your wife will be like a fruitful vine in your home, and your sons will be like young olive trees around your table. A man **who obeys the Lord** will surely be blessed like this."* (TEV)

The story of Daniel recorded in the Old Testament in a book by his name, is fascinating indeed. The setting is in the time of Babylonian captivity (605-538 B.C.). Daniel was among the captives taken from Jerusalem to Babylon. As an outsider, Daniel rose quickly to prominence under Nebuchadnezzar and subsequently, King Darius' rule, enough so to be challenged by his pagan cohorts/administrators. Daniel 6:1-5 lays it out for us: *". . . Then the presidents and satraps sought to find a ground for complaint against Daniel with regard to the kingdom; but they could find no ground for complaint or any fault because **he was faithful**, and no error or fault was found in him. Then these men said, 'We shall not find any ground for complaint against this Daniel unless we find it in connection with the law of his God.'"* (RSV) Truly God exalts those who are faithful to Him regardless of the setting!

In Hosea 4:1, the prophet declares, *"Hear the word of the Lord, O people of Israel; for the Lord has a controversy with the inhabitants of the land. There is **no faithfulness** or kindness, and no knowledge of God in the land; . . . ".* (RSV)

We will conclude our *dash* through the Old Testament with Proverbs 20:6 which highlights the rarity of faithfulness! *"Everyone talks about how loyal and faithful he is, but just try to find someone who really is!"* (TEV)

NEW TESTAMENT PASSAGES

Our New Testament survey on obedience and faithfulness will be easier, so to speak, if for no other reason than the sheer volume of the Old Testament writings. I will still need to be selective because the New Testament is fertile ground on these subjects. The starting point will be the Gospels, focusing on the words and ideas (the perspective) of Jesus on the matter at hand.

Jesus understood obedience as related to his earthly parents, Joseph and Mary. As the story goes, recorded in Luke 2:41-51, after one day's travel on their way home after observing the Passover Feast in Jerusalem, they realized that their twelve-year-old son was not with them. Sounds a bit strange to us but Luke explains that Joseph and Mary were traveling with a large group of relatives and friends – and kids will be kids! After looking among the group and not finding him, they headed back to Jerusalem. I cannot imagine them being *happy* about his absence. They found him in the Jewish Temple with the teachers, listening and asking questions. After expressing their consternation, Jesus responded in this manner: *"Why did you have to look for me? Didn't you know that I had to be in my Father's house (tending to my Father's business)?"* Mary and Joseph didn't understand what he was talking about at the moment but certainly knew their son, Jesus, was no ordinary child. The passage concludes with this statement about Jesus as a child, *"So Jesus went back with them to Nazareth, where he was* **obedient** *to them."* (Luke 2:51, TEV)

The Gospel of Matthew, Chapters 5-7, records Jesus' Sermon on the Mount in which He covers just about everything He deemed important. His message is lengthy, large in scope, and penetrating to the heart and minds of those following Him at the time and for all time to come. Matthew concludes the Sermon with this commentary on its impact: *"When Jesus finished saying these things, the crowd was amazed at the way he taught. He wasn't like the teachers of the Law; instead, he taught with authority."* (Matt. 7:28,29, TEV)

The final story Jesus told in his Sermon on the Mount was about two housebuilders, one **wise** and one **foolish**. It is worth re-telling here: *"So then, anyone who* **hears these words of mine and obeys** *them is like a wise man who built his house on the rock. The rain poured down, the rivers flooded over, and the wind blew hard against that house. But it did not fall, because it was built on rock. But anyone who* **hears these words of mine and does not obey** *them is like a foolish man who built his house on sand. The rain poured down, the rivers flooded over, the wind blew hard against that house, and it fell. And what a terrible fall that was!"* (Matthew 7:24-27 TEV)

The Gospel of John, chapters 13-17, records what transpired on Jesus' final night with the Twelve. When you think about it, everything He said to these men, his inner circle of disciples, must be considered of utmost importance. We can surmise it was deemed so by Jesus or He would not have spoken it. For purposes of this chapter, we will look only at one verse, John 14:21, *"Whoever accepts my commandments and* **obeys** *them, he is the one who* **loves** *me. My Father will love him who loves me; I too will love him and reveal myself to him."* (TEV) Verse 14:21 has only a slightly different focus than verse 14:23 which is included in chapter two's focus on the *Indwelling and Abiding* life. In reading John 14 one would have to be *deaf and dumb* to miss the connection between loving and obeying God.

Luke's description of the growth of the early church is instructive: *"And the Word of God increased, and the number of the disciples multiplied greatly in Jerusalem, and a great many of the (Jewish) priests were **obedient** to the faith."* (Acts 6:7 RSV) In essence, these priests with prominent positions in the Jewish culture of the day **disobeyed** the teaching that they were bound to teach, propagate, and abide by. Luke's choice of words describes accurately the position every follower of Christ must assume. **It is obedience as the foundation of our faith.** And it wasn't just a few. Luke says it was "a great many"! Can you imagine the personal price they paid for such a bold defection from the Jewish hierarchy of the day?

The Apostle Paul used similar language in the Introduction to his letter to the Romans. He begins by describing his position as a *"servant of Christ and an apostle"*. He continues with a detailed account of the person and work of *"Jesus Christ our Lord"*. (Acts 1:1-4 RSV) Verses 5 and 6 conclude his initial remarks, referring back to *"Jesus Christ our Lord, through whom we have received grace and apostleship to bring about the **obedience of faith** for the sake of his name among the nations, including yourselves who are called to belong to Jesus Christ."* (Acts 1:5,6 RSV) In Paul's mind being a faithful follower of Christ boiled down to one thing –obedience. Paul began his letter to the Roman Christians with a reference to *obedience* and he concludes his letter in Chapter 16 with the same emphasis: *"For while **your obedience** is known to all, so that I rejoice over you, I would have you wise as to what is good and guileless as to what is evil."* (Romans 16:19 RSV)

The New Testament Book of Hebrews is somewhat of an enigma concerning its authorship. Traditionally Paul was assumed to be the writer, but in more recent times that is in question. The recipients were Jewish Christians, so Barnabas, Paul's companion, a Jew, becomes a likely candidate. In reality, it is *"no le hace"* (Spanish for *"it does not matter"*)! Hebrews 5:8-9 is pertinent to this discussion. *"Although He (Jesus) was a Son, He learned **obedience** through what He suffered; and being made perfect He became the source of eternal salvation to all who **obey** Him."* (RSV)

The Apostle Peter is quite clear about the centrality of obedience for Christians in the first two verses of his brief letter. *"To the exiles of the Dispersion . . . chosen and destined by God the Father and sanctified by the Spirit for **obedience to Jesus Christ** and for sprinkling with His blood: May grace and peace be multiplied to you."* (I Peter 1:1, 2 RSV)

I am always touched by the Apostle Paul's way of ending his letters to the various churches. Without fail, his *endings* include the first names of dozens and dozens of individuals whom Paul deemed *faithful and obedient* followers and servants of Christ and his church. There are warm personal greetings and affirmations along the same lines in each of his letters. Here are a few examples. *"I recommend to you our sister Phoebe, who serves the church at Cenchreae . . . she has been a helper to many people and also to me . . . greetings to Pricilla and Aquila, my fellow workers in the service of Jesus Christ, they risked their lives for me . . . Ampliatus, my beloved in the Lord . . . the beloved Persis, who has worked hard in the Lord."* (Romans 16:1-10, RSV, TEV) Paul goes on and on through verse 16, referencing a few dozen more folks. I Corinthians 16 is a similar scenario. *"I am happy about the coming of Stephanas, and Achaicus, they have made up for your absence and have cheered me up, just as they cheered you up . . . the churches of Asia send greetings. Aquilla and Pricilla, together with the church in their house, send you hearty greetings in the Lord. All the brethren send greetings, Greet one another with a holy kiss."* (I Corinthians 16:17-20 RSV, TEV)

So why was Paul so successful in all his endeavors for the Lord? There are multiple reasons, but in reading his letters to the churches it is clear that his ministry was based upon personal relationships. Despite the warmth and cheeriness of his writings to the various churches, it is clear that his life was not void of conflicts and problems as evidenced by these words at the end of his letter to the Galatians. *"To conclude: let no one give me any more trouble, because the scars I have on my body show that I am the slave of Jesus. "* (Galatians 6:17 TEV) So what was true for Jesus was also true for one of His finest Apostles, Paul. Faithfulness and obedience inevitably involve suffering in one way or another.

CHAPTER 8

EVANGELISM AND SERVANTHOOD

Perhaps we should begin this chapter with a definition of terms to make the connection between *evangelist and servant* and the lives of ordinary followers of Christ. The teachings of Jesus and various other New Testament writers make it abundantly clear that the two-fold mission of all Christians at all times is the **proclamation of the Gospel** and **serving others at the point of their needs** be that the dramatic or the mundane. Both words are used as nouns and verbs. *"Evangelist"* translates the Greek word, *"euangelistes"*, which combines *"eu"* (good) and *"angelos"* (messenger). "Servant" translates the Greek word, *"doulos"* (a slave, a bondman, person of servile condition). Jesus Christ was the perfect example of both. As you work your way thru the New Testament you will discover that alternate expressions speak to the same reality. For example, Jesus' friend, The Apostle Peter, in a sermon early on in Acts, describes Jesus' ministry in this manner: *"You know the message God sent to the people of Israel, **proclaiming the Good News of peace through Jesus Christ**, who is Lord of all. You know of the great event that took*

*place throughout the land of Israel, beginning in Galilee after John preached his message of baptism. You know about **Jesus of Nazareth** and how God poured out on Him the Holy Spirit and power. He went about everywhere, **doing good and healing** all who were under the power of the Devil, for God was with him."* (Acts 10:36-38 TEV) This is Peter's way of saying that Jesus was a **servant** to those whom he encountered in the process of **proclaiming** the Good News.

Proclaiming the Gospel and being a servant is something you choose to do as an obedient follower of Jesus. The first eight chapters of the Gospel of Luke describe the early life and ministry of Jesus including his birth narrative, boyhood, baptism by John the Baptist, teaching, interactions with Jewish authorities, various miraculous healings and casting out of demons, and the calling of the Twelve Disciples who were firsthand witnesses to all He said and did.   Chapter Nine is a turning point. It records the very first time Jesus sent out his Disciples to do the kind of ministry they witnessed Him doing. In colloquial terms, it was their *first rodeo* so to speak! *Officially*, it was *The First Missionary Journey.* Here follow his instructions to them: *"Jesus called the twelve disciples together and gave them power and authority to drive out all demons and to cure diseases. Then he sent them out to preach the Kingdom of God and to heal the sick, after saying to them, 'Take nothing with you for the trip: no walking stick, no beggar's bag, no food, no money, not even an extra shirt. Wherever you are welcomed, stay in the same house until you leave that town; wherever people don't welcome you, leave that own and shake the dust off your feet as a warning to them.' The disciples left and traveled through all the villages, **preaching the Good news** (evangelizing) and healing (serving) people everywhere."* (Luke 9:1-6 TEV)

It seems that in Jesus' mind, evangelizing and serving were two sides of the same coin. They are intertwined in such a way as to be inseparable. Each one led to the other and vice versa. To serve someone at the point of their felt need often opens the door to being an evangelist to them, i.e. to share the Good News of Jesus with them. The real and felt need of many, many people in the first century was healing from disease and being delivered from demon possession. The Disciples were given power and authority to do both. As evidenced by Luke's testimony in verse six that is exactly what they did!

In our lives as twenty-first-century Christians, Jesus' words of empowerment and instruction are the same. What has changed is the setting. People still get sick but modern medicine handles most of those issues, and *demon possession* would not be a common malady in today's world. At least that's not what we'd call it! In today's world, the opportunity to be a witness and a servant for Jesus' sake is infinite.

The remainder of the New Testament is replete with passages that highlight personal evangelism and servanthood, and how they are related. However, before beginning a brief survey of key New Testament passages, I want to highlight a beautiful promise from the Psalms. *"The Lord is righteous and **loves good deeds**; those **who do them** will **live in His presence** (i.e.* abide in Him*)."* (Psalms 11:7 TEV) In choosing the following New Testament passages please note that in most cases the Scripture highlights servanthood and evangelism as stand-alone facets of the Christian life, e.g. Acts 1:8 TEV, which record Jesus' words of instruction to his Apostles after the Resurrection and right before the Ascension.

> *"But when the Holy Spirit comes upon you, you will be filled with power, and **you will be witnesses** (evangelists) for me Jerusalem, in all of Judea and Samaria, and to the ends of the earth."*

Regarding personal evangelism, I find it interesting that in one of the premier passages often quoted in sharing the Gospel, Ephesians 2:8,9, the last sentence of that paragraph is usually not included. *"For by grace you have been saved through faith, and this is not your own doing, it is the gift of God - not because of works, lest any man should boast."* The tenth verse that concludes the paragraph is as follows: ***"For we are his workmanship, created in Christ Jesus for good works, which God prepared beforehand, that we should walk in them."*** (Ephesians 2:10 RSV) Turns out in Paul's thinking salvation by the grace of God included a new life created by God that included *good works*!

I love Paul's description of his work in Thessalonica: *". . . as apostles of Christ, we could have made demands on you. But we were gentle when we were with you, like a mother taking care of her children. Because of our love for you, **we were ready to share with you not only the Good news from God but even our own lives.** You were so dear to us!"* (I

Thessalonians 2:7,8 TEV) Paul is often misunderstood as a tough, demanding, straight-talking preacher of the Gospel. Yes, he was tough under certain circumstances, but this passage highlights the real secret to his success as an ambassador for Christ. There was a tender side to Paul that endeared him to the people in the churches in which he visited and ministered. It is not a stretch to say the great evangelist, Paul, was also **a tender-hearted servant**.

As described in the introduction to Paul's *Letter to Titus* in the <u>Good News Bible</u> (TEV), *"Titus was a Gentile convert to Christianity who became a fellow worker and assistant to Paul in his missionary work."* Paul refers to him as his *"true son in the faith"*. (Titus 1:4 TEV) The letter includes instructions on a variety of practical issues for the church in Crete including basic expectations for church leaders, sound doctrine, and overall Christian conduct. About our focus of attention in this chapter, this small, three-chapter letter has four passages regarding servanthood. The first is addressed to Titus personally: "Show *yourself in all respects a model of good deeds . . ."* (Titus 2:7a RSV) *"Model"* translates Greek, *"tupon"* which simply means *"pattern"*. In personal terms, it refers to a person to be imitated, i.e., in this case, the pastor and/or leaders in the church on the island of Crete. God's people do need someone to go by, to pattern their lives after. I am a carpenter. I always draw up a plan, a pattern for me to follow when I am building something. My wife is a first-class seamstress, but without a pattern, she would be very limited as to what she could make. God expects those of us He calls as leaders to live the kind of lives that are worthy to serve as models, i.e., Christian ministry is a ministry of character as well as preaching and teaching. Paul was able to say do as I do, follow my example. Becoming a *model of good deeds* sounds a lot like the **Boy Scout Oath** of my youth: *"On my honor, I will do my best to do my duty to God and my country and to obey the Scout Law; **to help other people at all times**; to keep myself physically strong, mentally awake, and morally straight."* The **Boy Scout Law** includes being *"helpful to others without expecting a reward"*. One of Paul's main focuses in this letter to Titus is quite simply, practical Christianity, love-in-action, and doing servant kinds of things as a routine matter.

A few verses later in chapter two, Paul turns his attention to the church at large. The chapter concludes with a beautiful summary of the salvation story and a statement outlining the two-dimensional purpose of Jesus' self-sacrifice. *"For the grace of God has appeared for **the salvation of all men,** training us to renounce irreligion and worldly passions, and to live sober, upright, and godly lives in this world, awaiting our blessed hope, the appearing of the glory of our great God and Savior Jesus Christ, who gave himself for us to redeem us from all iniquity and to purify for himself **a people of his own who are zealous for good deeds."** (Titus 2:11-14 RSV) The focal word here is *zealous*. The question being, "what is our attitude when we do good deeds, acts of kindness. and selflessness?" Do we give ourselves joyfully or grudgingly, with enthusiasm or with reluctance? To be zealous is to be eager, to take the initiative, to look for opportunities to do good deeds, not just wait until they fall into your lap. Most people will not ask for help even when they need it; it is our place to see the need, take the initiative, and then respond accordingly. Jesus wants the world not only to hear with their ears, but also see with their eyes in our lives, the substance, character, and life-changing power of the Gospel.

The theme of *good deeds* continues in the final chapter three. *"I desire you to **insist on these things,** so that those who believe in God may be careful to **apply themselves to good deeds**; these are **excellent** and **profitable** for men."* (Titus 3:8 RSV) By using the word *"insist"*, is Paul suggesting that a lifestyle of applying oneself to good deeds is not even optional for the serious-minded Christian, for those of us who have believed in God and become his children? Yes, I think so. I am afraid that there is much more to being a Christian than most of us realize, much more expected of us as God's children than we would like to think. In some ways, our relationship with God is like a contract, an agreement between two parties. Over the last four decades or so, my wife and I have bought or built six homes. In each case, there was a contract involved between the two parties with specific stipulations for each. The terms are spelled out clearly in the contract, there is no leeway; you either meet the terms of the contract or pay the specified consequences. So it is with the Lord. There are terms to be met, specific "requirements", and expectations. On His part, we expect God to keep His promise to redeem us, and save us from our sins. He also promises to guide, protect, walk with us, and give us abundant life. But what about our side of the contract? What does He expect of us? The terms are simple but demanding and are found within His Holy Word. Implication? The better we know and live by His Word, the better we will keep our end of the bargain with the Lord. From our study of Paul's letter to Titus so far, we can conclude that one of the terms of our end of the contract is that we zealously apply ourselves to doing good deeds!

As if his point has not already been made, Paul reinforces it again in the next to last verse of his letter. *"And let our people **learn to apply themselves to good deeds,** so as to help **cases of urgent need,** and **not to be unfruitful."*** (Titus 3:14 RSV). Truth be known, this *learning* is an ongoing, life-long, never-ending process because doing for others, and being *other*-oriented is not a natural response for any of us. Our natural tendency is to live our lives wrapped up in, and focused on our own set of problems, in our small world. So doing good deeds is a learned behavior; hopefully, we will get better at it as we grow and mature in Christ. Paul offers two reasons for applying ourselves to doing good deeds. The first is to *"help cases of urgent need."* Some people need help. We can be part of the answer to their problems depending on our resources and gifts. The Lord wants us to minister to them as an ambassador of His love. The other reason for being a *doer of good* is somewhat negative. Simply speaking, we will be unfruitful, and our Father is not pleased with that.

Jesus taught in public venues to all those with ears to hear. At one point he said, *"Come to me, all who labor and are heavy laden, and I will give you rest. Take my yoke upon you and learn from me; for I am gentle and lowly in heart, and you will find rest for your souls. For my yoke is easy and my burden is light."* (Matthew 11: 29, 30 RSV) Decades ago I used to occasionally listen to Lester Roloff, 1914-1982, a fundamental, independent Baptist preacher who founded many homes for wayward teenagers across the South. His teaching was passionate, truthful, and offensive to many, but he is very intriguing to me. I remember an illustration he used in one of his sermons that has stayed with me over the years. He told of his childhood family farm and the mules his father used to pull the plows to cultivate their fields. It was his job to unhitch the mules from the plows at the end of the day. He recalled the scars on the backs of the mules where the yoke lay. He used this illustration to make the point that when you are yoked up with Jesus to do his work on this earth there are likely to be scars. In Paul's letter to the Galatians, in

74

conclusion, he said, *"Henceforth let no man trouble me; **for I bear in my body the marks of Jesus**. The grace of our Lord Jesus Christ be with your spirit, brethren. Amen."* (Galatians 6:17,18 RSV) Paul was not speaking metaphorically regarding his suffering for Jesus' sake. In his second letter to the Corinthian church, he enumerates his life as a servant of Christ: *"Are they servants of Christ? I am a better one — I am talking like a madman — with far greater labors, far more imprisonments, with countless beatings, and often near death. Five times I have received from the Jews the forty lashes less one. Three times I have been beaten with rods: once I was stoned. Three times I have been shipwrecked; a night and a day I have been adrift at sea; on frequent journeys, in danger from rivers, danger from robbers, danger from my own people, danger from Gentiles, danger in the city, danger in the wilderness, danger at sea, danger from false brethren; in toil and hardship, through many a sleepless night, in hunger and thirst, often without food, in cold and exposure. And, apart from other things, there is the daily pressure upon me of my anxiety for all the churches."* (II Corinthians 11:23-25 RSV)

Concluding this chapter is a segment of Jesus' Sermon on the Mount, and a summary statement of Jesus' public ministry from Matthew: *"You are the light of the world. A city on a hill cannot be hidden. Nor do men light a lamp and put it under a bushel, but on a stand, and it gives light to all in the house. Let your light so shine before men, that **they may see your good works and give glory to your Father who is in heaven**."* (Matthew 5:14-16 RSV) *"Jesus went around visiting all the towns and villages. **He taught in the synagogues, preached the Good News about the Kingdom, and healed people with every kind of disease and sickness**."* (Matthew 9:35 TEV) Jesus was doing exactly what he had asked his Disciples to do. Families bear a strong resemblance to each other; children are made in the image of their parents. Jesus is our Elder Brother in the family of God, so it is quite natural for us to want to be like Him. Evangelists and servants! Point made!

CHAPTER NINE

PERSONAL MINISTRY

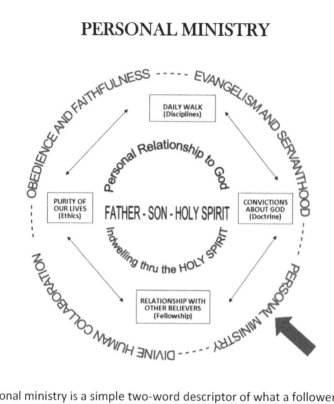

Personal ministry is a simple two-word descriptor of what a follower of Christ does with his/her life in the context of being an evangelist and a servant. It is something one does over a lifetime and very likely will change at various points. It is touching the lives of others inside and outside the Body of Christ with His love. Personal ministry is different for virtually every child of God and is shaped by one's gifts, preferences, strengths, weaknesses, personality, setting in life, family of origin, etc. One's ministry is rooted in vocation or calling which comes from God.

It is a common misunderstanding to limit *calling* and *vocation* to full-time Christian professionals, i.e. pastors, priests, etc. The truth is we are all called to be full-time in the ministry as *evangelists and servants* in our life situations whatever that might be. It is only a small minority of the family of God that is called to be full-time professionals. Here is a test: when you are doing the personal ministry God called you to do, you will be having the time of your life. It may be really hard work, and stressful, but you'll do it with a deep sense of satisfaction, gratification, and a smile on your face!

Understand that one's *personal ministry* happens both within and/or without one's chosen profession. My wife, Melva, is an educator and was blessed to practice her calling at all levels – from the university to elementary level, as a professor, teacher, and principal for 33 years. I bear personal witness that her profession as an educator was also the arena of her ministry for the Lord. You would only need to consult the dozens and dozens of teachers and thousands of students and parents to confirm my observation.

It will be helpful at this point to take a look at some basic teachings in the New Testament to guide our thinking. It is wise to never stray far from the bedrock teachings of Jesus in terms of defining ministry. Here's his "last" word on the topic, spoken to the Twelve: *"But it shall not be so among you; but whoever would be great among you must be your servant (Greek, diakonos), and whoever would be first among you must be slave (Greek, doulos) of all. For the Son of Man also came not to be served but to serve (Greek, diakonesai), and to give his life a ransom for many."* (Mark 10:43-45 RSV) Jesus uses two words to characterize their dealings with each other, one stronger than the other, servant and slave. And thus, the foundation of personal ministry begins with radical servanthood. That will always be the case. Jesus closes the conversation with a solemn reminder of his *personal ministry*: the giving of his life to save many others, the ultimate act of servanthood!

Paul's letters to various first-century churches comprise a significant portion of the New Testament. For our purposes, we will reference passages from only three of his letters – to the churches at Corinth, Ephesus, and Rome. In his second letter to the church at Corinth Paul corroborates Jesus' focus on self-denial/servanthood with this exhortation: *"And He (Jesus) died for all, that those who live (us!) might live **no longer for themselves** but for Him who for their sake died and was raised."* (II Corinthians 5:15 RSV) This is simply a small but important reminder embedded within a much larger and detailed recitation of basic Christian doctrine to this church in Corinth. For the larger context read II Corinthians in its entirety during your daily Quiet time!

To the church at Ephesus, Paul wrote: *"I therefore, a prisoner for the Lord, beg you to **lead a life worthy of the calling to which you have been called**, with all lowliness and meekness, with patience, forbearing one another in love, eager to maintain the unity of the Spirit in the bond of peace."* (Ephesians 4:1-3 RSV) A *life worthy* no doubt included personal ministry commensurate with one's *calling*. The Greek word translated *calling* is *klesis*. In the original American Standard Version of the New Testament, *klesis* is also translated as *vocation* which comes from the Latin word, *vocacio*; it is the participle form of the Latin *vocare* which means *to call*. The point is that *vocation* is not a New Testament word, but in the modern era, it is used to describe the same reality as one's *calling*. Parenthetically, Paul's letter to the Ephesian Christians carries a bit more weight when you consider that his calling, his *personal ministry*, has landed him in a Roman prison from which he is writing the letter!

In the following chapter, Paul expands the notion of God's call to include God's gifts. *"But grace was given to each of us according to the measure of **Christ's gift**. Therefore it is said, 'When He ascended on high he led a host of captives, and **he gave gifts to** men.' . . . And **his gifts** were that some should be apostles, some prophets, some evangelists, some pastors, and teachers, for the equipment of the saints, for the work of ministry, for building up the body of Christ, until we all attain to the unity of the faith and of the knowledge of the Son of God, to mature manhood, to the measure of the stature of the fullness of Christ. . . ."* (Ephesians 4:7, 8, 9-13a RSV) You may be thinking . . . "These words of Paul do not apply to me. I am none of the above." That would be true for most of us in the strictest sense of the word. However, we know by personal experience and observation that the Risen Christ's gifts to his brothers and sisters in the family of God are of endless variety and serve the very same noble purposes as outlined in verses 12 and 13. It becomes our responsibility to discern the gifts he has given and be about the business of using them for the sake of the body of Christ. That's another way of saying that we need to define our gifts and refine our efforts at having our unique personal ministry!

In his letter to the Church in Rome, Paul stays with the same theme but expands the nature of God's "gifts" in a refreshing way. *"For as in one body we have many members, and all the members do not have the same* *function, so we, though many, are one body in Christ, and individually members one of another. **Having gifts that differ** according to the grace given to us, let us use them: if prophecy, in proportion to our faith; if service, in our serving; he who teaches, in his teaching; he who exhorts, in his exhortation; he who contributes, in liberality; he who gives aid, with zeal; he who does acts of mercy, with cheerfulness."* (Romans 12:4-8, RSV) What a beautiful summary of giftedness within the Body of Christ. With a suggestive *list* like the above, we can all be assured that we have not been left outside the Lord's generosity in his giving of gifts to his children!

There is no better way to conclude this chapter on *personal ministry* than to present my story and the life stories of people I know and respect who are living out these principles. I have already referenced my wife and her vocation/calling as a Christian educator. If I narrowed it down to a few descriptors, my vocation/calling is/was a full-time campus minister as a leader, teacher, equipper, encourager, and servant of students at the graduate and undergraduate levels. My college years at Texas A&M were pivotal in my spiritual growth. Early on I was involved in two on-campus Christian ministries, Baptist Student Union and the Navigators. Being involved in both was untenable, so eventually, I decided to go with the Baptist Student Union ministry.

Between my junior and senior years, I served as a summer missionary in Nevada. That summer two important things happened. I met Melva Ann Neafus from Louisville, Kentucky, and I got well acquainted with Chet Reames, associate state BSU Director, who was in charge of the summer missions program. Late that summer, my BSU Director at Texas A&M, Prentiss Chunn, died. To cover the leadership gap, Chet traveled to College Station weekly for most of my senior year to meet with the BSU student leaders, me being one of them. He met with each of us personally, and I'll never forget one afternoon in my dorm room when Chet told me if ever I felt inclined to do Baptist campus ministry, to give him a call. About three years later, after I graduated from Southwest Baptist Theological Seminary with a Master of Divinity, I made that call and subsequently spent 24 years in campus ministry as a BSU Director on five campuses! In many respects, it was my friendship with Chet that God used to confirm my call.

That call expanded to a brand new arena for me in the late 1980s. It was late Saturday night and I was driving back to San Antonio on I-35 north of Laredo, Texas, with my wife and daughter in the truck with me. We were returning from a medical/dental mission trip to Nuevo Laredo, Mexico for a Friday/Saturday ministry in the colonias. The day was intense and filled with dramatic encounters with poor people being helped with serious medical and dental problems. I remember telling Melva and Jennifer that I felt called to lead medical/dental teams in Mexico regularly. It was just a year or so later that San Antonio CMDA began with me as the first Director. From that point forward we usually took at least seven such mission trips a year. My dream ministry/calling was fulfilled!

From 1977, when we moved to San Antonio to begin my ministry at UTSA and the UT HSC, and 2010, when I retired, I led approximately 150 medical/dental mission trips into Mexico, especially the border cities of Nuevo Laredo, Piedras Negras, and Ciudad Acuna. In that context, it was my great privilege to personally witness hundreds of Christians engaged in doing *personal ministry*. This included healthcare professionals of all descriptions, bilingual teachers from Melva's school, wheelchair repair technicians, University of Texas Health Science Center San Antonio students (medical, dental, nursing, physical and occupational therapy, etc.), and undergrads from UT San Antonio, Texas State University in San Marcos, and as far away as Texas A&M in College Station. As the leader of this ministry, it became clear to me that Christians were starving for opportunities to engage in *personal ministry*. The response was overwhelming, to the point that we would have to cut off registration at somewhere between 75 and 100 participants, depending upon the specific scope of a particular trip. We would recruit as many MDs and DDSs to adequately staff the scheduled sites. For undergrads, it would be as simple as limiting each campus to one carload.

I have to confess it is pure pleasure to lead a ministry that is so *right* in terms of purpose in which folks seek out the opportunity to participate. There was no recruitment per se. My task was simply to announce the date, and then watch the Lord go to work in putting together a team for that particular trip. I am most likely giving the reader the wrong impression that these trips were *easy* for me. However, for those of us who had various leadership roles, these trips required a great deal of organization and plain old hard work. A month or so before each mission trip, I made a pre-trip visit to the city in Mexico to get our border crossing set up as well as all the arrangements with the hosting pastors. There was the long car trip down Friday night, late night preparations, an early start Saturday morning, the ministry/work itself that lasted until late Saturday afternoon, then the long trip back from the border to San Antonio Saturday night.

For a clearer picture of this ministry, I would be remiss if I didn't briefly introduce you to a few of the people involved with me in these endeavors. David Singleton, DDS, who lived in White Oak, Texas, had a very successful dental practice and had been on several medical/dental mission trips sponsored by the Texas Baptist River Ministry. From a colleague, he heard about what was happening in San Antonio with CMDA regarding more frequent medical/dental mission trips to the Mexican border. After much prayer and consideration, he decided to sell his East Texas dental practice and move to San Antonio to follow his dream of *personal ministry* on border mission trips! I have no idea how many trips David and I did together . . . he did not miss many!

The challenge for me is singling out a very small sample of the hundreds of people involved across the spectrum of healthcare professionals and students, interpreters, helpers, and spouses . . . but let's begin.

One important facet of the border mission trips, especially to Piedras Negras, was what was termed our *wheelchair ministry*. The wheelchair ministry began in an unusual manner that underlines the Divine-human dimension. I met Javier and Rhonda Estrada on an airplane between San Antonio and Atlanta. I was headed to the national CMDA staff meeting in Bristol, Tennesee; they were going to Indiana to visit with her family for Christmas. Not too far into the flight, we got acquainted. It turns out Javier was a local pastor in Piedras Negras, and Rhonda was a registered nurse. Piedras Negras was one of our bi-annual medical/dental mission trip sites. After I shared with them the nature of our medical-dental border ministry, it was decided that their church would host one of our teams coming up in January. In the course of our conversation, I discovered that they had a personal relationship with the Mayor of Piedras Negras and his wife, who was in charge of the DIF (*Sistema Desarrollo*

82

Integral de la Familia), i.e. social services for the city. One of the huge needs in all the border cities we visited was helping the handicapped and disabled. One of our founding members of CMDA San Antonio, and a Council member, was Donald Currie, MD, professor of Rehabilitation Medicine at the UT SA Medical School. Don was a perfect fit for our wheelchair ministry. Need meets resource. There is no market in the United States for used wheelchairs and other devices. Over the years Don had been warehousing used wheelchairs in an empty garage space at one of his rent houses. His *stash* was huge! In addition, Don was connected to a network of professional wheelchair technicians in San Antonio whose job was to put together custom-fitted wheelchairs for people in need. So over the years, we went to Piedras Negras twice annually, and each time hosted a large wheelchair ministry at the DIF facility in the center of town. We witnessed families bringing their children, sometimes carried in the mother's arms, and in two or three hours roll out in a custom-fit wheelchair worth thousands of US dollars for free!

And it all started with a providential, chance encounter on a plane trip to CMDA headquarters. After twenty-five years that ministry is still flourishing. During those years my wife was the principal at Esparza Elementary a predominantly Hispanic neighborhood on the west side of San Antonio. Therefore, many of her faculty members were bilingual, and we always needed interpreters on our trips . . . again, need meets resource. Proficiency in a foreign language became the avenue for a very significant *personal ministry* for those teachers and spouses. Such was the case for Felipe and Jeane Tamez and Carlos and Mary Alice Ramirez. They were four of many of Melva's faculty who served the Lord on our trips as interpreters.

An aside. Word got out among the mayors of Mexican cities close to the Frontera (international border) about our medical and dental teams from San Antonio. On one Saturday in Piedras Negras, we were met by a delegation, including the mayor, from Nueva Rosita, a city about seventy miles into the interior. They implored us to bring our team to their city which we did in subsequent years after a preview visit with one major difference. Because of the distance, a weekend trip was not feasible so we scheduled a five-day trip during the following Spring Break. Jorge Guajardo was the mayor. On that first trip, the city housed our group in a very nice hotel and fed us every meal. That represents the depths of their gratitude. Our primary focus was the children attending a school for handicapped children as well as several other more remote church/clinic locations in the area.

I have mentioned one MD and one DDS by name so far. With each one stands a myriad of others who faithfully pursued their *personal ministry* calling as part of my CMDA ministry in San Antonio. Some were in private practice; others were faculty at the UTHSC San Antonio Medical and Dental Schools. One local MD deserves special recognition. I would be remiss to leave him out. When we began CMDA SA, Wayne Grant, MD, was the first Chairman of our local CMDA Board. Wayne was a local pediatrician, member, and Deacon at Trinity Baptist Church San Antonio, and already had extensive experience with medical/dental mission trips associated with the Texas Baptist River Ministry. What Wayne brought to the table was the practical experience in medical/dental border ministries which were already a major facet of his *personal ministry* long before CMDA came along.

From 1977 until 1994 I was the Baptist Student Union Director at the University of Texas San Antonio and the University of Texas Health Science Center San Antonio. There were many strongly committed Christians in those groups over the years, but one student stands out concerning a very specific calling to personal ministry. During his college years at UTSA, Mark Perkins was involved in BSU, and a member of our leadership team, the BSU Council. He felt a call to the ministry during his tenure at UTSA, and after his undergraduate degree, he enrolled in Southwestern Baptist Theological Seminary to pursue a Master of Divinity. As an undergraduate Mark Perkins always demonstrated a strong and clear call to personal evangelism. His seminary experience confirmed that calling. For the last 20 years, Mark has served as a full-time missionary in England. Besides preaching in various churches, and leading retreats, his primary assignment is *knocking on doors, cold turkey* evangelism, and presenting the Gospel to anyone who opens their door to him. Sounds like a tough assignment to most of us, but for Mark, it is pure pleasure because every day he gets to fulfill his very specific *personal ministry* calling - evangelism. After all these years, it is our privilege to be a part of his financial support team as one of our former students and friend.

I had the great honor and privilege of serving undergraduate and graduate students for forty-one years at six different campuses in two cities, Ft. Worth and San Antonio as a BSU Director and for the last sixteen years as CMDA Director for San Antonio and the UT HSC SA. One common feature of our ministries at each of those campuses included weekly, on-campus noon luncheons. This was no small task as we regularly had up to 300 students attending those weekly luncheons at two campuses. During the initial years of the CMDA luncheons at the UT HSC beginning in 1994, our average attendance was 175-225 students and staff. Virtually all the food for all those luncheons was provided by ladies' groups representing local churches. The food was paid for by the churches and prepared by the *noon luncheon* ladies, many of whom became dear friends of mine. For many of those 41 years, it was the Women's Missionary Union (WMU) from local Baptist churches. When CMDA SA came into being we reached out to other denominations with enthusiastic support as well. For the ladies (and a few men) who served those students faithfully for all those years, it was a very *personal ministry*.

As part of my profession and calling, beginning in the fall of 1977, medical, dental, and nursing students and spouses from the UT HSC were invited to our home on Tuesday nights for supper and Bible study – supper from 6:00-6:45 pm, Bible study from 6:45-7:30 pm. Initially, before she became an elementary school principal, my wife played the primary role in the planning and preparation of the meal. It was no small task as we regularly had 20-40 in attendance. In a very real sense that work was a significant part of Melva's *personal ministry*. Once her career in education moved from part-time to full-time, as a part-time professor at UTSA, a teacher with the NISD, and finally principal at Esparza Elementary, playing the lead role for the student suppers was no longer possible.

I have always enjoyed cooking and was pretty good at it, but I was swimming in deep water preparing suppers for 30-40 students every Tuesday night. That dimension of servanthood turned out to be a comfortable and enjoyable *personal ministry* for me over the years. When Araceli Adame, a dental student from the Lower Rio Grande Valley, told me she really liked my *carne guisada* made with my venison, it made my day! In the ensuing months when her fiancé, Matt Grunkemeyer, needed a place to stay during his orthopedic residency, he stayed with us for those three months. At that point, we were empty nesters with empty bedrooms . . . another avenue of *personal ministry* for Melva and me.

Conclusion

The reality is that for each of us, our personal ministry is an ever-expanding, multi-faceted adventure with the Lord. The possibilities are limitless.

The Apostle Paul says it as well as it can be said. . " . . . *I, therefore . . . beg you to live a life worthy of the calling to which you have been called* . . " (Ephesians 4:1, TEV)

There is *no one size fits all* description for *personal ministry* because every child of God is uniquely made, uniquely gifted, and called to live a life of *personal ministry* to His honor and glory.

CHAPTER TEN

DIVINE - human COLLABORATION

If anything is ever accomplished for the sake of the Kingdom of God, it is always the result of *Divine-human collaboration*. It is a phrase I have coined over the years to describe my experiences in ministry. It has been more of a discovery and realization rather than something I learned in seminary . . . more of an observation in retrospect than a strategy.

Numerous passages of Scripture would lead to that conclusion. However, there are at least three that state the reality in plain, direct terms.

*"**You** led your people like a shepherd, with **Moses and Aaron** in charge."* (Psalm 77:20 TEV)

"I am the true vine, and my Father is the vinedresser. Every branch of mine that bears no fruit, He takes away, and every branch that does bear fruit He prunes, that it may bear more fruit. Abide in me, and I in you. As the branch cannot bear fruit by itself, unless it abides in the vine, neither can you, unless you abide in me. I am the vine, you are the branches. He who

*abides in me, and I in him, he it is that bears much fruit, for **apart from me you can do nothing**."*   (John 15:1-5 RSV)

*"After all, who is Apollos? And who is Paul? We are simply servants, by whom you were led to believe. Each one of us does the work the Lord gave him to do; **I planted** the seed, **Apollos watered** the plant, but it was **God who made the plant grow**. The one who plants and the one who waters really do not matter. It is God who matters, for he makes the plant grow. There is no difference between the man who plants and the man who waters; God will reward each one according to the work he has done. For **we are partners working together for God**, and you are God's field."* (I Corinthians 3:5-9 TEV)

There is an obvious reason for the capitalization of the **D** in the phrase. The above passages bear that out. The human factor is always secondary to the Divine. Always!

In Psalm 77:20, the author, Asaph, makes a declarative statement concerning God's leadership, the Divine component, and then clarifies the reality on the ground as far as the people were concerned. Moses and Aaron were the visible expressions of God's leadership. The Scripture is simply a true statement of reality – God led his people and he used two capable men as his instruments, Moses and Aaron. They were tuned in to God's voice of instruction; in New Testament terms, they were no doubt *abiding* in Him. It was as Solomon states clearly in Proverbs 16:9, *"A **man's mind** plans his way, but the **Lord directs** his steps"*. (RSV)

The larger context of John 15:1-3 is John 13-17, Jesus' final instructions to the twelve men who would carry forth His ministry upon his *unexpected* Crucifixion and death. The venue was the Last Supper. Everything Jesus said that night should be studied, memorized, and lived to the best of our abilities. This passage is not necessarily any more important than the rest of what Jesus said, but it is a very important reminder of the central tenant of this final chapter of **Putting It All Together**. He was leaving his disciples physically, but not really, His resurrected self would continue to be present to them in the person of the Holy Spirit.

In John, Chapter 15, Jesus begins with a very familiar illustration from nature – the grapevine, which was a common feature of the landscape in

Palestine. If you break off a branch from the vine, it will not produce grapes and it will not survive. The point of a grapevine is to produce fruit, grapes, which then are turned into wine. Branches of the grapevine that do not produce grapes are pruned by the vinedresser. The underlying point of the metaphor seems to be the expectation of fruitfulness for grapevines and God's sons and daughters. It seems to me that Jesus is making an obvious and uncomfortable point with this teaching to none other than his chosen Twelve disciples. One's connection to the True Vine, i.e. Jesus, is simply a matter of *abiding in Him* daily. So we best understand clearly what the abiding relationship with Jesus is in plain, simple terms. It is only in the abiding that we can hope to be fruitful and live up to his expectations summarized in Jesus' concluding remarks: *"This is how my Father's glory is shown: by your bearing much fruit; and in this way you become my disciples."* (John 15:8 TEV)

In the previous chapter (14), Jesus makes connections between love, obedience, and abiding in Him. He says, *"If a man loves me* (step one), *he will obey* (step two) *my message."* The result: *"My Father will love him, and my Father and I will come to him and live with him (make our home with him).* (John 14:23, TEV, RSV) What an astounding announcement on Jesus' part! Loving and obeying leads to being indwelled by the Eternal God and his Son, Jesus, and that all happens through the agency of the Holy Spirit. (John 14:15-17 RSV) This may sound complicated but in reality, it is quite simple. We try to make it more difficult than it is. This is not to say that loving Him and obeying Him is *easy*, but it is not complicated!

What you have in I Corinthians 3:5-9 is a clear example laid out by Paul of the principle stated so well by Jesus in John's Gospel. It is about fruitfulness, husbandry in a human garden, and the church at Corinth. The members of the church seemed determined to focus on one or another person as responsible for their conversion and the establishment of their church, etc. In chapter three Paul puts an end to all that nonsense. The principals mentioned, Apollos and Paul, were simply equals, instruments of the Divine, behind the scenes . . . Yes, there was an initial "planting" of the Gospel seed by Paul, and subsequent "nurturing and watering" by Apollos, but neither had the wherewithal to produce growth and change. The human factor according to Paul was of minimal import and would be rewarded appropriately. Paul and Apollos were simply *partners working together for God.*

SO WHAT DOES THIS LOOK LIKE IN REAL LIFE IN THE 21ST CENTURY?

The principal characters have not changed even a little bit, not one *iota (the name for the ninth letter of the Greek alphabet, i, an extremely small amount)*. The Divine dimension is constant. Today's Christians operate on the same stage as first-century Christians like Paul and Apollos. Yes, the world has changed immensely, but all the same rules and principles of Divine-human collaboration apply.

I may have majored in Mathematics at Texas A&M, but over my forty-one years in campus ministry, I lost count long ago of instances where the final result or product of *my efforts* went way beyond my input and expectations. That fact never ceased to amaze and surprise me. No matter how hard or how smart I worked for the Lord, the final result was always way beyond my imagined consequences.

DEVELOPING A CITY-WIDE BSU MINISTRY

My tenure as a full-time Baptist Student Union Director began in the fall of 1970. I was given a ministry that had never happened before – develop a city-wide BSU ministry in Ft. Worth, Texas involving three campuses, Texas Wesleyan College and Tarrant County Junior Colleges Northeast and South campuses. I had three weekly on-campus Noon meetings and three BSU Councils (leadership teams) with 20+ individuals with whom I had a personal weekly conference. In addition, we had a city-wide Tuesday night meeting for the combined campuses meeting in the fellowship hall of Broadway Baptist Church (downtown, center city), Fall and Spring weekend retreats, state BSU meetings in the Fall and Spring, and a week-long mission trip during the winter break somewhere in South Texas . . . . . was this ministry a lot of work? To be sure, it was a lot of work. Was it worth it? Absolutely! Why was the final result after seven years of work way beyond my expectations and imagination? Because of the Divine-human *formula.* Whatever efforts I made, however smart I may have been . . . no matter. It was always about the *capital D, lowercase h* phenomenon. Whatever efforts I made were always overshadowed by God's blessing and enrichment.

GOD'S LUMBERYARD

Ft. Worth BSU, early 1970's, a Saturday mission project with my students. Early on in my student ministries, I maintained a strong focus on servanthood. One of the features of that aspect of the ministry was what I called *Servant Seminars*. They began Saturday morning early and ended that night. I would contact pastors of churches with lots of elderly members and get a list of home projects we could do that day to lend a hand with whatever they needed us to do. In one case, the need was for us to build a wheelchair access ramp for the back door/porch. Two of my guys were experienced carpenters, Wayland Roberts and Mike Eason, so building it was no big deal . . . an easy job for them. The challenge was that we had no lumber and no money to buy it. It was a low-budget operation! I happened to notice that directly across the street was a pile of used lumber left by a contractor to be thrown away. Again, need meets resource! Only God could arrange that kind of deal! Yes, I planned the *Servant Seminar*, and I lined up the projects, but I had absolutely nothing to do with providing the needed lumber for the wheelchair ramp. And the amount of lumber for the ramp was not just adequate, it was way beyond what was needed! Gracias a Dios! Without being reckless, sometimes it is necessary to just put yourself out there in a vulnerable position and let the Good Lord do HIS THING! Be it providing lumber or enabling one to speak *fluent Spanish* when needed!

DEVELOPING A LOCAL CMDA MINISTRY IN SAN ANTONIO

Jump to 1994. In July of that year, I resigned from my position as a BSU Director (24 years total) at UTSA and the UTHSCSA (18 years) to begin a brand new ministry for the Christian Medical and Dental Association. The job was to initiate a city-wide, locally-funded CMDA ministry in San Antonio for healthcare professionals and students at the University of Texas Health Science Center.

The new CMDA ministry officially began on campus in September 1994. For the previous seven years, I had been hosting a noon luncheon on campus under the banner of the Baptist Student Union, averaging 75 in attendance. It was a denominationally supported/funded ministry, funded by local Baptists, and was quite successful.

I was in for a shock. We hosted our first CMDA Welcome Party at our house, about two miles from the campus, which we called a *Fajita Extravaganza*. I grilled 35 #'s beef fajitas and 20 #'s chicken breasts! Then there were beans, Spanish rice, pico de gallo, etc. It was quite a party! The newly formed San Antonio CMDA Council (professionals) and the Student Leadership team helped with all the preparations. To our great surprise and delight, 150+ students and spouses came to that first CMDA gathering at our home! We had cars everywhere if you can imagine it. Our neighbors were most kind and in all the years that students came to our home, there was never even one complaint. That was the beginning of CMDA San Antonio – only the beginning.

At our on-campus Thursday noon luncheon, we immediately started having 200+ attending. On more than one occasion, people were sitting on the steps in the aisles. Our *Noon Luncheon Ladies* from local churches were thrilled at the response. They never once complained about the numbers. They were caught up in the excitement and student response. The immediate success of San Antonio CMDA was never about me or the other folks in leadership positions. We were not bystanders to be sure, but something was happening in the ministry that went way beyond our efforts. That was always obvious to me. The San Antonio CMDA ministry momentum never ebbed for the 16 years I was Director and has continued to this day. I knew and all my key people, students, and professionals knew that this was a *God thing*. The national CMDA staff was astounded by the success of this first locally funded CMDA ministry in the USA. It was the first and there were many to follow – to date, hundreds. San Antonio CMDA continues to be the largest and the only ministry with two full-time staff. We were never fooled by our vanity. As with Paul and Apollos, all of us knew *we were working together with God*. It was He that produced such an abundant and beautiful harvest!

THE BROKEN COLLARBONE

In the early years of our border medical/dental mission trips, Ken Long, MD, from San Marcos, Texas, was one of our regular, faithful partners. We counted on him for every trip. His very first trip with us was to one of the colonias in Nuevo Laredo, Mexico. Early that Saturday morning a teenager showed up at Ken's clinic site (a room in someone's home) complaining of arm and shoulder pain. Ken quickly diagnosed the problem – a broken collarbone. It had happened the day before, but his parents had not taken him to the hospital for treatment. Ken set the broken collarbone back in place, fabricated a cross-chest sling to stabilize the broken bone, and sent him on his way. Need meets resource in a poorer-than-usual colonia on the backside of nowhere. That was Ken's first patient on his first trip with us. It was not his last! I guess the Good Lord brought that teenager to Dr. Long for both their sakes.

THE TRIP TO EL POTRERO

Cecilio and Araceli lived in that same colonia in Nuevo Laredo and for several years they hosted a medical clinic in their humble home. Cecilio was a pastor and their home also doubled as a church. On one of our mission trips, they informed us that they would be moving about three hours south of the border to El Potrero, a small town near Bustamonte in the state of Nuevo Leon. Cecilio was to become pastor of the evangelical church in El Potrero. They invited us to bring a medical and dental team to work in their community. This was before the widespread use of cell phones, so when we decided to make an exploratory trip to El Potrero and check out the possibilities, it was somewhat of a leap of faith. Kellie Hooker, Associate CMDA Director at the time, Marta Villareal who was a good friend of Cecilio and Araceli, with Spanish being her native tongue, Keith Patteson, a third-year medical student, and I made the trip. All we knew was that Cecilio pastored a church in El Potrero. We had no address or phone connection. In essence, we were depending on the Lord to help us find them. When we arrived in El Potrero late in the afternoon, we just started asking questions and after several conversations determined the location of his church and their home. In talking with neighbors it was determined that they were out of town, but would be back in the morning. So we arranged with the neighbors to tell them that we would be back early the next morning. We headed to Bustamante, the closest town that would have some type of accommodations for the night. We had a rather comical experience at the hotel restaurant. They gave each of us menus, but as we gave them our orders, they kept saying they didn't have what we were ordering. Finally, we asked, "*What do you have*"? The answer was *"cabrito de orno"*, baked goat.   So that's what we had for our supper.

The next morning happened to be Parents' Day at the local school, so they invited us to join them.   In the providence of God, the one person that we needed to meet on the trip was the mayor's wife.   She was the one person who could make arrangements for our medical and dental teams, and also get permission for us to cross the border and safe passage into the interior.   So everything fell into place and for the next couple of years, we took medical and dental teams to El Potrero.   Considering that we initially *struck out in the blind* on that exploratory trip, it became obvious to us that the Lord was way ahead of us, opening doors, arranging needed encounters, etc.   The Divine-human partnership worked perfectly!

SPEAKING WITH CUSTOMS OFFICER

The setting is the International Bridge at Del Rio/Ciudad Acuna.   The occasion was a CMDA medical-dental mission trip to Cd. Acuna, Mexico.   I was crossing the border with a team and it was before the times when we began getting permission beforehand from the Aduana (Customs) to cross with our team and equipment.   This time we were stopped by one of the border guards, holding us up for no good reason.   We were already running a bit late.   Please understand, I had taken Spanish in high school and college, but I was nowhere near to being fluent, and had not had that much opportunity to speak Spanish regularly.   Nevertheless, I got out of the truck and began to speak fluent Spanish with his man for at least five minutes.   At the end of our *conversation*, he simply said to me, *pasale*, which means, *you can go*!   I got back in the truck and said to the folks riding with me, *"I have no idea what just happened.   I just spoke fluent Spanish to him and I don't know what I said."*   It was like the Good Lord gave me the gift of tongues for five minutes – it was a God thing, not Roger!

THE EXTRA PROSTHETIC LEG

It was late Thursday afternoon at our wheelchair storage garage.   We were loading our trailer with used wheelchairs, parts, and various other rehab ministry resources to take to Piedras Negras, Mexico the following day.   We came across a prosthetic right leg, above the knee.   The question was asked, *"Should we take this? Chances are slim we can use it."* After a short discussion, my answer was, *"Sure, why not, you never know what we might need."* So the prosthetic leg was loaded in the trailer. Saturday morning in Piedras Negras our rehab team, led by Dr. Don Currie, was seeing patients, especially children needing custom wheelchairs. Mid-morning a grown man walked into our clinic on crutches, his right leg amputated just above the knee! Yep, you guessed it. That prosthetic leg was a perfect fit! My wife, Melva, was on that particular trip and it was her great privilege to customize a pad to fit his leg. Again, the need meets the resource in a ministry context. The Good Lord knew all along that man would be coming to our clinic. We did not have a clue. The Lord prompted us to take that prosthetic leg with us, and that man walked out on two legs! His life changed forever! What a privilege it is to partner with Him in ministry and our lives!

PRISON DENTISTRY

Piedras Negras, Mexico is the site of a high-security federal prison that houses both men and women. Our local contact informed me that there was a great need for a dentist, more specifically, an oral surgeon for extractions. It was a potentially dangerous assignment. I decided to take a very small team – Tom McAnear, DDS/MD, oral surgeon, a male upperclassman dental student as his assistant, Marta Villareal, an older woman who had made many trips to minister to the women prisoners on previous occasions, and myself as the *Jefe* to work with the prison officials. Marta was a Hispanic woman with a passion for personal evangelism, sharing the Gospel with almost everyone she encountered, fearless in the face of any possible dangers. This was not her first visit to this prison.

When we got into the prison, we had no idea that it would be open with hundreds of male prisoners just standing around, gawking at us as we made our way to the clinic site which was simply an empty room. Was the setting threatening? Certainly. Were we afraid? I would say no. I reckon the Good Lord gave each of us an inner sense of His Presence, protection, and peace. Without the conviction that we were there as His emissaries, none of us, except maybe Martha, would have mustered the courage to be there. It was clear in our hearts and minds that we were *partnering with Him* on a Divine assignment. There were no incidents, we all got out safely, and a great many prisoners were relieved of chronic pain from bad teeth extracted by Dr. McAnear's skilled hands. In addition, several of the women prisoners accepted the Lord that day in response to Marta's witness much to our delight!

CONCLUSION

The Christian life is a rather complex mixture of the personal and the corporate, devotion and doing, listening and speaking, and personal and Divine participation. Our success as a child of God depends upon how well we navigate the complexities and learn to live in the secure confidence of our **Divine-human partnership**. When you are working as a partner with Almighty God, ordinary mathematics do not apply. In His arena, 1 + 1 rarely equals 2! In my experience, the number could be 4, 6, 8, or even 10! It has happened so many times, I must confess, I am no longer surprised. My hope and prayer is that in reading this book you will find clarity, knowledge, and motivation to walk with the Father as a fruitful and joyful member of His Great Family which comprises His Great Kingdom.

CONCLUSION

It is my hope and prayer that my attempt to organize and formalize accepted beliefs about Christian theology, doctrine, and practice have helped you.

As stressed earlier a mindset of intentionality is needed if you are to implement the particulars of the **Putting It All Together Model** in your daily life. If you venture to implement some of these ideas and begin to incorporate new habits, disciplines, practical tools, and new ways of thinking and living, I can assure you that you will experience a definite impact on your relationship with the living God and his Son, Jesus.

PRACTICAL TOOLS AND RELATED MATERIALS

I. KEEPING A SPIRITUAL JOURNAL

INTRODUCTION

My first Journal entry was on April 26, 1966. I was a twenty-year-old Junior at Texas A&M. It was written on 3 ½" x 6 ½" notebook paper kept in a tiny black spiral notebook. The note at the top says, *"Began* (i.e my journal) *after reading Manna in the Morning".* Here is my very first entry, unedited, *"felt wonderful today – a little doubt still about the method – Lord showed me I badly needed understanding for Christian guys not living for Jesus – looking forward to good day knowing the Lord is with me".* My self-proclaimed title for my journal was simply – *"Between Me and God".* I have come a long way since that humble, sincere beginning. This morning my daily entry was on page 3,838! I have used leather-bound Journal notebooks for a good long time. After Bible reading, prayers of petition, and intercession, my quiet time concludes with a journal entry. The journal routine and entries have been refined over the decades, but they are consistent with my original, untutored intention – it remains, *"Between me and God"*!
I heartily recommend this daily discipline to those so inclined.

A WORKING DEFINITION

A personal spiritual journal is a written record of the inner dialogue of a person and him/herself and the Living God. It is like writing our book as *we* happen. A journal is a place where spiritual growth is privately nourished. Journals are often begun at the turning points of life such as one's college years, or the beginning of any significant life-altering venture. In one way or another, the journal answers the ever-present question, *"Who am I at this point in my life?"* [32]

---

[32] Simons, George F. Keeping Your Personal Journal. New York: Paulist Press, 1978. Pp. 10-12

REASONS FOR KEEPING A SPIRITUAL JOURNAL [33]

1. The journal is a place to record important events so we do not forget them. It has a way of giving continuity to our lives.
2. Journaling provides a concrete, creative way of dialoguing with an unseen Friend.
3. It allows our creativity and imagination to have free rein.
4. It provides a middle way of expressing our emotions between repression and explosive action.
5. One's journal offers a forum for objectivity in dealing with our emotions.
6. The journal can be a valuable therapeutic instrument in coping with sorrows, fears, struggles, - inner turmoil.
7. The journal facilitates personal growth and increases self-knowledge.
8. Journalling deepens our relationship with the Father as we reflect on the Scripture and our experience of life in Him.

BENEFITS

There are several basic means of keeping our spiritual equilibrium such as involvement in a local church, honest sharing with trusted friends, spending time alone for prayer, silence, Scripture reading, study, and meditation. The personal spiritual journal has a way of tying all these elements together. Morton Kelsey says it well:

> *"Outside of my friends and guides along the religious way, my journal-keeping has helped more to bring my life together and set me on the religious way than any other one religious practice. It has kept me honest, given me companionship, and allowed me to listen to the deepest levels of myself, allowed me to vent my deepest anger, and brought me into creative, saving relationship with . . . a Divine Lover . . ."* [34]

---

[33] Kelsey, Morton T. Companions On The Inner Way. New York: Crossroad, 1984. Pp. 130-134.
[34] Kelsey, pp. 129-130.

PRACTICAL SUGGESTIONS

1. Purchase a separate journal or notebook or designate a section in your spiritual notebook for that purpose. If you choose the second option you will need to create a file for your journal pages. A good rule of thumb is to keep no more than ten completed pages in the notebook at any one time. A file folder will enable you to preserve your writing for future reference. It is important, however, to safeguard your privacy by whatever means that is appropriate.

2. Begin each entry with the date time, and place, making special notation if you are doing something out of your ordinary routine like attending a conference or retreat, on vacation, etc.

3. Consider combining your daily "to-do" *lists* and prayer concerns in the same notebook as your journal.

4. For persons with a weight problem, a daily food diary is a helpful companion tool for weight control. That is simply a matter of writing down everything you eat and recording the approximate number of calories if you seriously want to lose weight. It can be kept at the beginning of the personal journal. The primary benefit of a food diary is awareness of the kind and quantity of food you are eating. Since *you are what you eat*, this additional discipline can make a very positive contribution to your physical health and a general sense of well-being.

5. The nature of your journal entries over a year might include:
   - written prayers – *"Dear Father . . . "*
      - reflection on your general state of being – physical, emotional, spiritual, relational, etc.
   - writing poems or songs as you are inspired or making drawings
   - expressing strong emotions – love, anger, fear, sorrow, joy
   - recording in diary fashion the important events of your life
   - recording dreams that seem significant to you

6. Remember that consistency is more important than the length of your journal entries.

7. For an in-depth treatment of this topic I recommend reading Keeping Your Personal Journal by George F. Simons.

EXERCISES – GETTING STARTED[35]

1. A BEGINNING – For the first week, make a daily journal entry regardless of how you feel about it. Focus on the expression of your feelings and your interaction with Scripture. Write out at least one prayer.

2. TIME – Take a fresh page in your journal and draw the face of a clock, without hands. As you look at the clock, ask yourself the question, "*What time is it in my life?*" Think about it for a while, then draw in the minute and hour hands. Write a descriptive paragraph beginning with a statement like this *"It's nine o'clock in the morning and . . .".* Use the following questions to further assist your exploration of time in your life.

   - It is too late to . . .
   - It is too soon to . . .
   - I need time for . . .
   - I expect that _____ will happen at _____ oclock.
   - An alarm is set for _____ o'clock. It means . . .

3. DEATH AND REBIRTH: SEASONS OF THE SOUL – The motifs of death and resurrection are at the very heart of Christianity.

   • Begin this exercise by making a list of at least five things in your life that are dying, diminishing, becoming less important, receding, separating, the things you are losing interest in, letting go of, and things that seem just about over. Think in terms of relationships, hobbies, passions, interests, commitments, etc.
   • Make a second list of five or so things that are on the rise in your life, ascending, coming into being, emerging, returning, becoming more important, more desirable, etc.
   • After making your lists, meditate on them for a while and then pick one item from each list that seems most important, and then write a paragraph about each for entry into your journal.

4. COMPENSATIONS – Each of us makes compensations of some kind because they seem to be of advantage to us. Some compensations come from an unhealthy self-image. We compensate to make up for what we perceive to be our inadequacies. This exercise is intended to help you understand some of your compensations.

---

[35] Simons, pp. 106-132

Begin by identifying some of the inadequacies or handicaps which you would ordinarily see yourself as having. Jot them down in your journal. Use these categories to stimulate your thinking:

- Age – I am too old/young to . . .
- Sex – I am a man/woman, but only women/men are allowed to . . .
- Social background – If I were white/black/rich/etc., I would . . .
- Possessions – If I had _____, I could . . .
- Personal physical appearance/constitution – I am too short/tall/weak/etc., to . . .
- Mental, emotional, motor skills – I am too dumb/afraid/awkward/etc., to . . .

5. DESTINATIONS: A ROAD MAP – Draw a map of the places you intend to go in terms of your personal and career objectives. Draw in the route you have taken, including the detours and side trips. Mark the spot where you are at present. In your journal entry explore your feelings about where you have been, and not been, and where you are planning to go.

6. THREE PORTRAITS – Use three pages of your journal to draw three pictures of yourself. At the top of each page write one of these captions: "I was", "I am", or "I will be". These represent yourself in the past, present, and future. Feel free to use words, sketches, symbols, or whatever suits you to make these drawings. In your journal describe your responses to each of your drawings.

7. MATTERS OF LIFE AND DEATH - Answer the following questions in your journal:

- Who or what am I willing to live for?
- Who or what is killing me?
- Who or what do I want to be more alive for?
- Who or what am I willing to die for?

8. SOCIAL CIRCLES – On a page in your journal draw circles representing the groups, organizations, and collections of people to whom you belong formally or in formally, by birth or by choice. Write a reflection based on your feelings about each of these groups, especially at the points where they overlap and even conflict.

9. TREATIES – We all have agreements, treaties, spoken or unspoken, in the important relationships of our lives. Pick out one person, perhaps your best friend, and identify the terms of your treaty together. What are your expectations of each other? What happens when one of the parties breaks the terms of your treaty? What would you like to change about your treaty?

10. SOUL GENEALOGIES – Most of us can trace our ancestry back several generations, but what about your soul genealogy? Who were the people who have sired you spiritually? Who are the people who have inspired, believed in, encouraged, prayed for, delighted in, and walked beside you up to this point in your life? Take a substantial amount of time and trace your spiritual heritage in as much detail as you can. Follow this journal exercise with letters of appreciation if you feel so inclined.

SOURCES

Companions On The Inner Way by Morton T. Kelsey
The Journal of John Wesley, edited by Percy Livingston
Keeping your personal Journal by George F. Simons
The Journal of John Woolman edited by Frederick B. Tolles

II. DEVELOPING A LIFELONG PLAN FOR PERSONAL BIBLE STUDY

I. PRELIMINARY CONSIDERATIONS

- The foremost consideration is the attitude of your heart, i.e., your level of motivation regarding personal Bible study.
  - Scripture: Psalm 119:16-24,33-36,47-48,92-93, 97-103,111-112,127-131,165 Jeremiah 15:16
  - In your time alone with God this week honestly face the question of motivation for personal Bible study.
  - Any Bible study plan is of little value in the hands of an unmotivated person.

- The second most important consideration is your uniqueness as a child of God.
  - It will be up to your initiative to select from these materials and elsewhere, ideas that are well-suited to your individual needs and circumstances.
  - There is no magic plan that will work for everyone. You must make a plan work for you.

- You do need a plan - your plan. Without one, you will wander aimlessly through life in terms of Bible study and consequently be ill-equipped for effective Christian living.

- In developing a lifelong plan of personal Bible study, it is important to keep in mind that the whole Bible is the inspired Word of God, and therefore worthy of your study. However, although all portions are equally inspired, they are not all equally relevant to daily Christian living.

A lifelong plan should include a balance between reading, studying, meditation, and memorization.

II. BASIC PRINCIPLES

- Because the Bible is characterized by levels of relevance, some portions should receive greater priority than others. Historically, the Psalms and the four Gospels have been given that priority. Implications:
  - Read and/or study the Psalms and Gospels on alternate days, weeks, or months year-round.
  - Read straight through the Old and New Testaments concurrently (excluding the Psalms and Gospels), on alternate days, weeks, or months.

- For the sake of variety, utilize various methods of personal Bible study.
- Use a standard translation as your basic study text such as the *New American Standard Version*, or the *New International Version*. Each of these translations is published as a study Bible that includes various helpful features such as a Concordance.

- Take advantage of modern Biblical scholarship by using various modern translations
  either as a single concentration for one year or concurrently. e.g. *Today's English Version, J.B. Phillips Translation*.

  Personal Note: My parents gave me a *Revised Standard Version* of the Bible after my baptism at age ten. As a result, I have used the RSV consistently for most of my life as a standard translation similar to the New American Standard and New Internation versions. During my college years, I started using the *Today's English Version* translation was first published in 1966. It is subtitled *Good News for Modern Man*. To the present, this is the Bible translation I primarily use for my daily quiet time.

- In the course of your study, as the God of the Bible meets you, inspires you, and convicts you, memorize those portions that are especially meaningful.

- Keep in mind that your usefulness to the Father in the work of his Kingdom is to some extent dependent upon your level of excellence in being a lifelong student of his Word.

III. METHODS FOR PERSONAL BIBLE STUDY

Introduction

Studying the Bible goes beyond reading the Bible and it is important to develop a plan for such. Years ago a friend recommended a book by Richard Warren entitled 12 Dynamic Bible Study Methods. I found this book helpful in my student ministry in developing a curriculum for a course I developed called *Discipleship 101*. One of the aspects of the course was helping students become *students* of the Bible. In this section, I have chosen four of the twelve methods presented in the book – the Devotional, Chapter Summary, Topical, and Biographical methods. For each method, I will provide an overview/definition, an example, and an outline to follow when doing one yourself.[36]

The Devotional Method

Definition: The devotional method involves taking a passage of the Bible and prayerfully meditating on it until the Holy Spirit helps you apply its truth to your life in a way that is personal, practical, possible, and provable. The goal is for you to take the Word of God seriously and therefore to be obedient to the God of the Bible.

Meditation: Meditation is the key to discovering how to apply Scripture to your life. It is essentially thought digestion. You take a thought that God gives you, put it in your mind, and think about it over and over again. It will help to paraphrase or outline the passage under consideration. Read the verses in a modern translation such as Today's English Version or the New International Version.

---

[36] Warren, Richard. 12 Dynamic Bible Study Methods. S P Publications Inc., 1981. Note: The descriptions in this section of the four Bible study methods chosen are summaries of material in Warren's book; the method outlines are taken from the book, and the study examples are from the author's personal Bible study.

The following questions help meditate on a passage (not all questions are relevant to every passage):

Is there any . . .

. . . sin to confess	. . . promise to claim
. . . attitude to change	. . . command to obey
. . . example to follow	. . . prayer to pray
. . . error to avoid	. . . truth to believe
. . . things to praise or thank God for?	

Application: God never intended for the Bible to merely be interpreted. It must be applied to our daily living if God's purpose for His Word is to be realized. He gave us the Bible to show us how we can have a personal relationship with Him and how we are to live in His way in His world.

Four Suggestions for Good Application:

1. Make it Personal.

2. Make it Practical.

3. Make it Possible.

4. Make it Provable.

Devotional Bible Study - Format

Date: Passage:

1. Pray for insight into the passage and read it in several translations if possible.

2. Meditation (paraphrase or outline the passage to get at the meaning):

3. Personal Application:

4. Key Verse for Memory:

Devotional Bible Study – Example

Date: Passage:
Philippians 1: 9-11

1. Prayer for insight.

2. Meditation (outline)

> This is a prayer of Paul's for the Christians at Phillipi.
>
> He has one basic request with three results. The request – That their love (agape) increase, i.e., the love that God supplies to them, and that it be informed and discerning love.
>
> Three results:
>
> - That they will be able to sort things out in light of the highest priorities – *recognize the highest and the best.*
> - That they will be morally pure – live righteous, holy, blameless lives.
> - That they will be filled with the fruits of righteousness, i.e., positive goodness, which is produced by the power that Christ gives and results in His being glorified.

3. Personal Application

> By changing this prayer to first person, it would be suitable for me to pray daily.
>
> The only way for God's love to increase in my life is for me to open more of myself to Him, e.g., like opening a window to let a cool breeze in.
>
> By doing this I will do better concerning:
> My sense of values/priorities
> The moral purity of my life
> The positive goodness in my life
> (*All of the above can use some improvement!*)

4. Key verse for memory: the entire passage.

Chapter Summary Method

Introduction: The Bible as originally written had no chapter or verse divisions. It was not until A. D. 1228 that Bishop Stephen Langton added the chapter divisions. Even though some of the divisions are arbitrary and tend to interrupt the flow of the writer's message, in most cases, they are appropriate and provide good breaking points which are helpful in Bible study.

Definition: This method involves gaining a general understanding of the contents of a chapter of the Bible by reading it through at least five times in several translations, asking a series of content questions, summarizing the central thoughts, and making personal applications.

Advantages: It is easy to learn and does not require a great amount of time to do. No outside help or reference tools are needed. It can be incorporated into a personal plan of reading through the Bible.

Tips for Reading the Chapter:
1. Read in a Bible without notes so as not to influence your impressions.
2. Read without stopping. Do not concentrate on details at first. Try to catch the central theme.
3. Read in several different modern translations.
4. Read the chapter aloud once.

Ten Steps in a Chapter Summary Bible Study:
1. **Title** – give the chapter a short descriptive title.
2. **Outline or Summarize the contents** – the method will depend largely on the literary style of the chapter.
3. **Important people** – list them.
4. **Choice verse(s)** – write out the verse for future reference.
5. **Keywords** – list them
6. **Problems, Questions** – If any arise in your study write them down and ask someone for clarification.
7. **Cross References** – look up in your study Bible other passages that may shed light on the chapter.
8. **Insight Into the Person of God** – what have you learned as a result of studying this chapter?
9. **Central Lesson(s)** – write out your main impressions.
10. **Personal Application** – remember to apply the same criteria here as in the devotional method.

Chapter Summary Bible Study - Format

Location of Chapter:

Read Five Times: Check When done.

1. Title

2. Outline, Summary, or Paraphrase of Contents:

3. Important People:

4. Choice Verse(s):

5. Key Word(s):

6. Problems, Questions Raised:

7. Cross References:

8. Insights into the person of God (Father, Son, or Holy Spirit):

9. Central Lesson(s):

10. Personal; Application:

Chapter Summary Bible Study – Example

CHAPTER: Psalm 19   **Read five times:** yes

1. **Title:** "God, His Creation, and His Word"

2. **Outline and Summary of Contents:**

   I. God's Glory in Creation (vs. 1 6)

God made this world and universe in such a way that it inevitably bears witness to his personhood. You cannot experience life without receiving a rather clear message about God from creation. His character is written into the "warp and woof" of the natural order.

   II. God's Word in Revelation (vs. 7-11)   Even more definitive than God's self-revelation in nature is His revelation through the written Word. His Word is perfect, sure, right, pure, clean, true, just, eternal, and fair. His Word revives the soul, gives wisdom, makes people happy, and gives understanding and knowledge.

   III. God's Children in Their Weakness (vs. 12-14)   There are two kinds of sin - unconscious and deliberate. All of us sin without wanting to or even knowing that we sin. We are highly skilled at self-deception and we need each other's help with this problem. We also sin very deliberately willfully and on purpose. When that kind of sin gets out of hand we are no longer in control of our lives. Rather we are being controlled by sin itself.

3. **Important People:** God

4. **Choice Verses:** 19:1,7 11,12 14

5. **Key Words:** God's glory, law (word) of the Lord, perfect, strength, trustworthy, wisdom, right, happy, just, understanding, fair, desirable, hidden faults.

6. **Problems, Questions Raised:**
   •   Does the Word of God as revealed in nature speak clearly enough to make accountable those who have not heard the Gospel?

- Can we assume a one-to-one correspondence between the "law, testimony, precepts, commandments, ordinances of the Lord" and the Word of the Lord as we know it in the Bible?

7. **Cross References:** Romans 1:19 23, Isaiah 40:12 31, Psalm 119, Psalm 139:23,24, Jeremiah 15:16. Joshua 1:8

8. **Insights into the person of God:**
   - God is a God of self-revelation.
   - He reveals himself in nature and through His Word in a way that can be comprehended.
   - He cares about us and wants to know us personally.

9. **Central lessons:**
   - God's glory is very evident in His natural creation.
   - God's written Word is as glorious as His *natural* Word.
   - There are many benefits to being a serious student of the Bible.
   - Human beings are weak indeed, desperately in need of God's help to keep free from sin - deliberate or otherwise.

10. **Personal application:**
    - I will continue my lifelong pattern of experiencing God in his creation.
    - I will take seriously my being a student of the Bible because of the benefits to gain from such exposure to God through his Word.
    - I will be aware of my tendency toward self-deception regarding sin,   and will openly solicit feedback from Christian brothers and sisters to break through the veil of my deception and be less inclined toward unconscious sin.
    - I will make Psalm 19:14 a consistent prayer of my life.

Topical Method

Definition: This method involves selecting a biblical subject and tracing it through a single book, the Old or New Testament, or the entire Bible to discover what God says about the topic. It uses extensive cross-referencing and the questions you ask of a given text are limitless.

Importance of this method:

1. It enables you to study the Bible systematically and logically.

2. It gives you proper perspective and balance regarding biblical truth. You get to see comprehensive biblical teaching on a given subject.

3. It allows you to study subjects that are of particular interest to you.

4. It provides a vehicle for studying the great doctrines of the Bible.

5. It lends itself to good and lively discussions. The results of a topical study are always easy to share with others.

6. It allows you variety in your lifetime commitment to personal Bible study. The number of topics is inexhaustible.

Helpful Tools:

1. A study Bible – e.g. Thompson's Chain Reference Bible, The NIV Study Bible, New International Version, Zondervan.

2. A Concordance – should be in the back of any good study Bible.

3. A topical Bible – e.g. Knave's Topical Bible or The New Compact Topical Bible by Zondervan.

Suggestions:
1. Be systematic – Do not try to study the Bible in a haphazard, undisciplined manner.
2. Be thorough – Find and study as many verses as possible that relate to the topic.
3. Be exact – Carefully determine the meaning of each verse you study, avoiding taking verses out of context.

Topical Bible Study - Format

Topic Under Consideration:

1. Compile a list of words related to the topic:

2. Collect Bible References:

Comparison Chart

3. Consider each reference individually:

4. Compare and group the references in appropriate categories:

Reference   Cross Reference   Insights

5. Condensed Outline:

6. Conclusions (summary and application)

Topical Bible Study – Example

TOPIC: Faithfulness

1. **List of related words:**
   - fidelity
   - utterly dependable
   - reliable
   - worthy of being trusted to carry out one's responsibility

2. Bible references:

Old Testament
Deuteronomy 32:4
I Samuel 2:35
II Chronicles 31:20
Psalm 12:1; 31:23; 40:10
89:2; 117:2; 119:90
Proverbs 20:6
Nehemiah 9:8
Isaiah 25:1
Daniel 6:4
Lamentations 3:21 24
Hosea 4:1

New Testament
Matthew 24:45 51; 25:14 30
Acts 11:23
I Corin. 1:9;4:2;10:13
Galatians 5:22
Colossians 1:7
I Thessalonians 5:24
II Thessalonians 3:3
II Timothy 2:2
Revelation 2:10; 19:11

3. Old Testament Reference   Insights/Observations

Deuteronomy 32:4 - A verse about the character of God, our *mighty defender*; perfect, just in all his ways, He does what is right and fair, faithful and true.

I Samuel 2:35   The Lord reveals his desires for the type of priest to serve Him and minister to the people   "*This priest will be faithful to God and do everything God wants him to*".

II Chronicles 31:20,21 (II Chronicles 16:9) A comment on the character of King Hezekiah "*He did what was good and right and faithful before the Lord his God*".(RSV) vs. 21 "*He was successful because everything he did for the Lord he did in a spirit of complete loyalty and devotion to his God*". This verse links success and faithfulness.

Psalm 12:1 "*Help, Lord, for there is no longer anyone that is godly; for the faithful have vanished from among the sons of men*". (RSV)   A cry of anguish over the lack of the faithful in the land.

Psalm 31:23 "*Love the Lord, all his faithful people. The Lord protects the faithful.*" This verse links faith¬fulness and God's protection.

Psalm 40:10 *"I have spoken always of your faithfulness and help"*. It is an appropriate part of our sharing with others to tell them about the faithfulness of our God.

Psalm 89:2 TEV *"I know that your love will last for all time, that your faithfulness is as permanent as the sky."* This verse testifies to the certainty of God's faithfulness.

Psalm 117:2 Same theme as the above verse. *"Great is his steadfast love toward us, and the faithfulness of the Lord endures forever. Praise the Lord!"*

Psalm 119:90 Same theme as above. *"Your faithfulness endures through all the ages; You have set the earth in place and it remains".*

Proverbs 20:6 *"Many a man proclaims his own loyalty, but a faithful man who can find?"* (RSV) *"Everyone talks about how faithful and loyal he is, but just try to find someone who really is!"* (TEV) This verse talks about the relative scarcity of truly faithful people.

Isaiah 25:1 (Numbers 23:19) *"Lord, you are my God; I will honor you and praise your name. You have done amazing things; you have faithfully carried out the plans you made long ago."* Testifies to God's utter dependability.

Daniel 6:4 Daniel was a faithful man to his responsibilities. None of his enemies could find fault with him.

Hosea 4:1 3 The Lord's accusation: *"There is no faithful¬ness or love in the land, and the people do not acknowledge me as God."* It continues, *"They make promises and break them; they lie, murder, steal, and commit adultery. Crimes increase and there is one murder after another. And so the land will dry up, and everything that lives on it will die. All the animals and birds and even the fish will die."* This is a rather dim future for an atheistic nation such as ours.

Nehemiah 9:8 A comment about Abraham and God's faithful¬ness: *"You (God) found that Abraham was faithful to you, and you made a covenant with him... the Promised Land ... where his descendants would live. You kept your promise because you are faithful."* Therefore, the implication is that God makes covenants with faithful people.

Lamentations 3:21 24   A despairing man recalls God's faithfulness: *"Hope returns when I remember this one thing   The Lord's unfailing love and mercy still continue, fresh as the morning, as sure as the sunrise. Great is thy faithfulness. `The Lord is my portion, says my soul, `therefore I will hope in Him."* This is a beautiful statement of hope and faith and commitment based on God's faithfulness.

4. New Testament Reference Insights/Observations

Matthew 24:45 51   Compares the faithful (reward) and unfaithful (punishment) servant. The faithful servant is busy doing his master's work. The master is very harsh toward the unfaithful servant who ignores and abuses his responsibility. Synonyms would be obedient and dis¬obedient and good versus evil.

Matthew 25:14 30   Compares three servants, two who successfully managed the master's assets and one who sat on the assets given. The first two were called "good and faithful" because they wisely used their God-given assets. Compared here is action versus inaction, hard-working versus lazy, and vulnerable versus safe.

I Corinthians 4:2   Faithfulness is the one requirement for a servant to his master. Phillips translates "faithful" in this verse as "worthy of trust".

Galatians 5:22   Faithfulness (Phillips fidelity) is listed as one of the fruits of the Holy Spirit.

Acts 11:23   Barnabus exhorts the church at Antioch to be faithful and true to the Lord with all their hearts. Phillips, *"Be resolute in their faithfulness to the Lord"*.

I Corinthians 1:9   Verse affirms God's faithfulness. Phillips translates the verse *"God is utterly dependable."*

I Corinthians 10:13   God is faithful to his children in the face of temptation. Phillips, *"God can be trusted."*

II Timothy 2:2   One of the goals of evangelism is to entrust the Gospel with faithful (Phillips *"reliable"*) men who will pass it on to others.

Colossians 1:7   Epaphras is characterized as Christ's faithful worker.

I Thessalonians 5:24   God is faithful. He will do what He promises.

II Thessalonians 3:3 *"The Lord is utterly faithful He will strengthen and keep you safe from the Evil One"*. (RSV) Phillips, *"God will finish what He has set out to do."*

Revelation 19:11 A vision of Jesus on a white horse. He is called faithful and true.

5. Condensed Outline

I. God's Faithfulness
   A. God's faithfulness is certain. There is never any question about it.
   B. His demands on his children to be faithful are based upon his faithfulness to them. (i.e. rooted in his character).
   C. God's faithfulness can be a real source of encouragement when we are depressed.
   D. God's Holy Spirit is at work in believers to produce faithfulness.
   E. God rewards faithfulness and punishes unfaith¬fulness.
   F. Personal evangelism involves sharing about God's faithfulness.

II. Man's Faithfulness
   A. Faithfulness is one of the primary requirements for pleasing God as one of his children/servants.
   B. Faithfulness to God involves the wise use of God-given assets and resources.
   C. Faithfulness means fulfilling God-given responsibilities.
   D. True faithfulness is a scarce commodity even among the people o God.
   E. Good examples of faithfulness:
      1. Old Testament Abraham, Daniel, and King Hezekiah
      2. New Testament Paul, John, Peter, Epaphras

6. Application

- This study has forced me to evaluate my faithfulness since the Scripture says so much about its importance to God.
- I find myself with a renewed appreciation of God's faithfulness to me after this study.
- This study has greatly increased my awareness of the negative effects of unfaithfulness.
- I must evaluate my faithfulness on this basis:

- o   My use of my God-given assets/resources.
- o   My fulfilling God-given responsibilities.
- Those are God's criteria for grading my faithfulness to Him.
- My goal is to be one of the persons whom God considers faithful, i.e., someone He can depend on me to do his work on this earth.

7.. Verses to be memorized:

Old Testament	New Testament
Deuteronomy 32:4	I Corinthians 1:9
II Chronicles 31:20,21	I Corinthians 4:2
II Chronicles 16:9	II Timothy 2:2
Psalm 89:2	
Proverbs 20:6	
Hosea 4:1 3	
Isaiah 25:1	
Nehemiah 9:8	

Biographical Method

Importance of People in the Bible: It is almost trite to say that people are important to God; they are made in his image and his book, the Bible, is a record of his dealings with men and women throughout history. You cannot fully appreciate the Bible until you get to know the people of the Bible.

Much of the Old Testament is in narrative form, describing the lives of many people in graphic detail. From these narratives, much can be learned by way of examples, both good and bad. The New Testament is more of an equal blend between narrative and instruction. In many cases, New Testament truths are illustrated in the lives of Old Testament characters.

There are approximately 3,000 persons mentioned in Scripture. This Bible study method opens wide the door for meaningful, exciting, and fulfilling personal Bible study.

Tools Needed: In doing a biographical Bible study it will be helpful to have a study Bible, a concordance, several translations of Scripture, and a topical Bible.

Tips for a Good Biographical Study:

1. Start with a person on whom you can do a relatively simple study.

2. Do your best to *live with* the person you are studying. Walk in his/her sandals. Try to get inside that person's mind and discover how he/she thinks, feels, and responds to life.

3. Be careful not to confuse different people in the Bible who have the same name, e.g., John the Baptist, John the Beloved Disciple, and John Mark.

4. Be aware that some people in the Bible have multiple names, e.g., Peter/Simon/Cephas.

5. Do your biblical studies on a person before referring to materials written by others about that person, i.e., do primary research.

124

Biographical Bible Study - Format

1. Name:

2. Scripture References:

3. First Impressions/Observations:

4. Outline his/her life:

5. General Insights:

6. Character Qualities Identified:

7. Bible Truths Illustrated in His/Her life:

8. Summary of Lessons Learned from His/Her Life:

9. Personal Application:

10, Transferable Concepts (things I can share with others):

11. Someone with whom I can share this study:

Biographical Bible Study – Example

1. **Name:** Mary of Bethany
2. **Scripture References:** Mark 14:3-9, Matthew 21:17, Luke 10:38-42, John 12:3, John 11:1, Matthew 26:6-13

3. **First Impressions/Observations:**
   - Seemed to be a significant person in Jesus' life.
   - She was one of the more significant women to whom He related as a friend.

4. **Outline of Her Life:** (Sketchy at best)
   - Sister of Martha and Lazarus
   - Had a deeply spiritual relationship with the Lord
   - Her home provided a place of refuge for the Lord
   - She was one of his closest friends
   - She was different from her sister in temperament

5. **General Insights:**
   - What did Jesus say about her? "She has done a beautiful thing for me; she will be remembered for it."
   - How did she handle a crisis? She handled the death of her brother in a normal fashion. (i.e. with grief)
   - Who were her close friends? Jesus Himself was one of them.
   - She likely had continual hassles with her sister over the household chores.

6. **Character Qualities Identified:**
   - thankful, grateful to God, and able to express it
   - compassionate to Jesus
   - knew how to be quiet and listen
   - insensitive to her sister
   - contemplative by nature
   - assertive in friendship

7. **Bible Truths Illustrated in Her Life:**
   - Romans 12:1 - *"With eyes wide open to the grace of God..."* - gratitude to God
   - Proverbs 8:17 - *"I love those who love me and those who seek me diligently find me."* - assertiveness in seeking God
   - Psalm 40:6 - *"You have given me an open ear..."* – desire to listen to God

8. **Summary of Lessons Learned from Her Life:**
   - Jesus indicated his approval of lavish expressions of gratitude to God. Therefore when it is authentic, it is also appropriate for any of God's children.
   - In Mary's life, Jesus affirms the priority of one's relationship with Him.
   - Even public figures need friendship.

9. **Personal Application:**
   - I need to look for appropriate and authentic ways of expressing my gratitude for what God has done for me.
   - I need to give absolute priority to my relationship with Him, and at the same time be comfortable with my uniqueness in terms of temperament.

10. **Transferable Concepts:**
   - Be lavish with your gratitude to God and others around you.
   - Be a listener as a child of God, not just a busybody.
   - Be willing to befriend public figures for their sake and yours.

11. **Someone with Whom I can Share This Study:**
   My BSU Student leaders

IV. SCRIPTURE MEMORY

I. MOTIVATION FOR SCRIPTURE MEMORY

- Love for God: Matthew 22:37 I Corinthians 13:2
- Respect for God and what He has said about his Word: II Timothy 3:16,17 Ephesians 6:10 17 Joshua 1:8 Psalm 119:105,130,165 Matthew 4:4
- Desire for spiritual growth: Ephesians 4:15 Philippians 3:12 14
- Hunger for God and his Word: Jeremiah 15:16 Psalm 119:1 7,14, 16,18,24,28,47,48,73,97 103, 111,112,127 131

II. HOW TO GET STARTED

- Decide that Scripture memory will be a priority in your life.
- Make a covenant of accountability with several other people.
- Set yourself a challenging yet attainable goal.
- Begin by learning verses with which you are already familiar.
- Learn a good set of verses on basic Christian doctrine, e.g., the person of Christ, sin, salvation, etc.
- Learn other verses that mean something to you from your personal Bible study.
- Consider learning paragraphs rather than individual verses.
- Write verses neatly on small cards (1 ¾" x 2 ¾") with the verse on one side and the reference on the other.
- Say verses out loud to yourself and review them with a friend.
- Make Scripture memory a part of your daily routine, e.g., while driving to school.
- Learn several verses on pride because often Scripture memory produces spiritual pride.
- Use discretion in sharing verses with others.

III. SUGGESTED SCRIPTURES

- Abiding in Christ   John 15:4,5

- Companions   Proverbs 13:20

- Fruits of the Holy Spirit   Galatians 5:22,23

- God's Word   II Timothy 3:16,17, Joshua 1:8,9, Jeremiah 15:16, Psalm 119:9- 11,105

- God's Provision for Man's Need I Peter 3:18, Romans 5:8,
  I John 5:11,12, John 14:6, I Timothy 2:5

- Man's Necessary Response John 1:12, Ephesians 2:8,9,
  Romans 10:9,10

- Man's Need Romans 3:23; 6:23, Isaiah 59:1,2

- Obedience John 14:23

- Prayer Luke 11:9,10, Hebrews 4:16, I John 5:14

- Peace of Mind Isaiah 26:3, John 16:33, Philippians 4:47

- Strength for Living Isaiah 40:28- 31, Psalm 73:26,
  II Corinthians 12:9, 10

- Forgiveness Psalm 51:10 13, I John 1:9

- Time Alone with God Mark 1:35

- Wisdom James 1:2 5

- Your Daily Walk

Wisdom from Proverbs
Note: The following verses are especially good in *Today's English Version*

- Confession 28:13

- Divine Human Collaboration 16:9

- Drinking, Gluttony 23:19 21, 29 35

- Faithfulness 20:6

- Giving 11:24,25

- God's Purposes 19:21

- God's Reward 22:4

- Honesty 24:26

- Irresponsible People 25:19

- Keeping Your Word 25:14

- Learning from Others 27:17

- Listening   18:2
- Marriage   18:22
- Mind and Body   14:30; 17:22
- Personal Growth   18:15 (TEV)
- Purity of Life   25:4
- Seeking Counsel   15:22
- The Way of Men   16:25
- Wisdom   24:5,6
- Your Heart, the Key   4:23

V. QUIET TIME - SUGGESTIONS

INTRODUCTION/DEFINITION

By *quiet time* I understand the term to mean a daily, designated, consistent, private time with the Lord. The specifics are entirely up to you – location, length of time, content – and depend upon your stage in life, your preferences, availability, life circumstances, etc.

About 33 years ago my father died, and as his eldest son and executor of his estate, the responsibility of taking care of his financial affairs fell primarily on my shoulders. With my two brothers' help, it took approximately five years to accomplish our goal. Early on it became obvious to me that this task was way beyond my/our human capacity. In response, I decided I needed more time for my *quiet time*. Because of our family circumstances, I begin a pattern of getting up at 5:15 am to have my QT and wake my wife at 6:00 am. That pattern suited me well and to this day I do the same except I wake my wife at 7:00 am, enabling me the freedom to have a longer and more leisurely QT.

There are three elements to my quiet time: Bible reading, prayer, and writing in my journal. The Bible reading and the journal aspects are covered in sections 1 and 2.

PRAYER

Before my prayers, I have found it helpful to read several classic writings that include: two Creeds, one benediction, and two prayers of relinquishment.

The Apostles' Creed
(the oldest form appeared in AD 340)

I believe in God, the Father Almighty, Creator of heaven and earth.
I believe in Jesus Christ, his only Son, our Lord who was conceived by the Holy Spirit, born of the Virgin Mary, suffered under Pontius Pilate, was crucified, died, and was buried; he descended to the dead.
On the third day, he rose again;
He ascended into Heaven, He is seated at the right hand of the Father, and He will come again to judge the living and the dead.
I believe in the Holy Spirit, the universal church as the Body of Christ, the fellowship of all believers, the forgiveness of sins, the resurrection of the body, and life everlasting.   Amen

The Nicene Creed
(original prayer was from the Council of Nicea in 325 AD)

We believe in one God, the Father, the Almighty, maker of heaven and
earth, of all that is, seen and unseen.

We believe in one Lord, Jesus Christ, the only Son of God. eternally
begotten of the Father,   God from God, Light from Light, true
God from true God, begotten not made, of one being with the
Father. Through Him, all things were made. For us and our
salvation, he came down from heaven: by the power of the Holy
Spirit, he became incarnate from the Virgin Mary and was made
man. For our sake he was crucified under Pontius Pilate; he
suffered death and was buried, On the third day he rose again in
accordance with the Scriptures; he ascended into heaven and is
seated at the right hand of the Father. He will come again in
glory to judge the living and the dead, and his Kingdom will have
no end.

We believe in the Holy Spirit, the Lord, the giver of life, who proceeds from
the Father and the Son. With the Father and the Son, He is
worshipped and glorified. He has spoken through the prophets.
We believe in one holy catholic and apostolic Church.
We acknowledge one baptism for the forgiveness of sins.
We look for the resurrection of the dead, and the life of the world
to come.

John Claypool's Benediction

Depart now in the Fellowship of God the Father,
and as you go remember:
In the Goodness of God you were born into this world;
By the Grace of God, you have been kept all the day long even to
this very hour;
By the Love of God, fully revealed in the Face of Jesus . . .
you are being . . . Redeemed.
(John Claypool, Baptist minister/Episcopal priest, 1930-2005)

Prayers of Relinquishment

"Lord, I am yours, I do yield myself up entirely to You, and believe that You do take me. I leave myself with You. Work in me all the good pleasure of your will, and I will only lie still in Your hands and trust You."[37]
(Hannah Whitall Smith, Early Quaker, 1832-1911)

"I am no longer mine, but Yours . . . I freely and wholeheartedly yield all things to Your pleasure and disposal. . . And now, glorious and blessed God, Father, Son, and Holy Spirit, You are mine, and I am Yours. So be it. And the covenant I have made on earth let it be ratified in Heaven. Amen"
(John Wesley, 1703-1781, A Covenant Prayer, selected portions.)

---

[37] Smith, Hannah Whitall. The Christian's Secret of a Happy Life. New Jersey: Revell Company, 1870, p. 67.

INTERCESSORY PRAYERS AND PRAYERS OF PETITIONS

I have found the following outlines helpful in organizing my intercessions and petitions. You can create your own or copy these. You will need a minimal supply of each because, as time passes, they will need to be updated, added to, etc. Life is not static!

INTERCESSORY PRAYERS

CLOSE FAMILY

OTHER FAMILY

CLOSE FRIENDS

SIGNIFICANT OTHERS

Sunday	**Thursday**
Monday	**Friday**
Tuesday	**Saturday**
Wednesday	

PETITIONS

Begin Date	Description	End Date

November 3, '22, Thursday, Boerne – Father of steadfast love, tender mercies, and amazing deeds of infinite wisdom, power, and perfect timing, I bless and praise You this new day. I offer myself to You for your blessing and protection. I offer my daily "sacrifice" of thanksgiving for all your gifts and kindnesses to me, "deserved, earned" and not, recognized as such and not . . . each and everyone, greatly appreciated. Please forgive my sins and shortcomings, deliver me from hidden faults, secret sins, pride, hypocrisy, and despair over our national affairs. Bless my day with my Dear Melva, help me to love, honor, cherish, and serve her at every opportunity. Order my time today, help me make good use of it. Guide my thinking, and therefore, my doing. Fill me with your Holy Spirit, Power, and the Fruit thereof – love, joy, peace, patience, kindness, goodness, faithfulness, gentleness, and self-control. May I abide in You, love, listen, and obey your Voice of instruction. And please, "make your home in me", Father, Son, and Holy Spirit, as promised by Jesus in John 14:23! Let it be according to me and mine according to your love, mercy, grace, wisdom, and power. In Jesus' name, I pray. Amen

Note: I often include other folks I'm praying for in my Journal entries, depending on timing, needs, etc. That wouldn't be appropriate in this particular entry.

VI. DIMENSIONS OF DISCIPLESHIP

This section is another attempt at *"putting it all together"* with a different construct using three gerunds, *knowing, being, and doing.* A gerund is defined as a word form that is derived from a verb but functions as a noun.

In my ministry to students, I was constantly looking for new ways to describe the Christian life. These three gerunds describe uniquely that journey. If you decided to categorize all the teachings in the Bible from Genesis to Revelation, they would fit into one of these three *categories.*

KNOWING

Key Word – Relationship (*with God*)

Key Question - Who do we know?

Relevant Scriptures

OT - Jeremiah 9:23,24

NT - Philippians 3:7,8; John 17:3

BEING

Key Word – Character (*the essence of who we are morally speaking*)

Key Question - Who are we?

Relevant Scriptures

OT - Exodus 20:1-19 (Ten Commandments)

NT - Matthew 5; Ephesians 4:11-15;

II Peter 1:3-8; II Corinthians 3:18

DOING

Key Word – Ministry (*the Great Commission, being a servant and evangelist*)

Key Question - What are we doing with our lives for God's Sake?

Relevant Scriptures

OT - Micah 6:8; Isaiah 58:1-11

NT - Luke 9:1-6; Acts 1:8; Mark 10:45;

Acts 10:38

VII. THE WILL OF GOD

FINDING GOD'S WILL - HEARING GOD'S VOICE - MAKING DECISIONS

Selected Scriptures - OT

Abraham - Genesis 12:1-2; 22:1,2 - "The LORD had said to Abram, "Leave your country, your people and your father's household and go to the land I will show you. . . Sometime later God tested Abraham. He said to him, "Abraham!" "Here I am," he replied. Then God said, "Take your son, your only son, Isaac, whom you love, and go to the region of Moriah. Sacrifice him there as a burnt offering on one of the mountains I will tell you about."

Moses - Exodus 3:1 - 4:17 - A conversation, a dialogue as God gave Moses his mission to be the one who delivered his people from Egyptian bondage.

Samuel - I Samuel 3:1-18 - A wake-up call from the Lord, a vision from the Lord as to his mission in life.

Joshua – Joshua 9:25 - "We are now in your hands. Do to us whatever seems good and right to you."

David - 1 Chronicles 13:1-4; 28:2,11,19 - "David conferred with each of his officers, the commanders of thousands and commanders of hundreds. He then said to the whole assembly of Israel, "If it seems good to you and if it is the will of the LORD our God, let us send word far and wide to the rest of our brothers throughout the territories of Israel, and also to the priests and Levites who are with them in their towns and pasture lands, to come and join us. Let us bring the ark of our God back to us, for we did not inquire of it during the reign of Saul." The whole assembly agreed to do this because it seemed right to all the people.

The Wisdom of **Solomon** - A warning - Proverbs 14:12 - "What you think is the right road, may lead to death."

Proverbs 15:22 - "Without counsel plans go wrong, but with many advisors, they succeed." RSV

Proverbs 16:9 - "A man/woman's mind plans his/her way, but God directs his/her steps." TEV

Proverbs 19:21 - "Many are the plans in the mind of a man/woman, but it is the purpose of the Lord that will be established." TEV

Selected Scriptures - NT

Luke 1:3 - "Therefore, since I have carefully investigated everything from the beginning, it seemed good also to me to write an orderly account for you, most excellent Theophilus. . . ."

Luke 1:5-20 - The Lord speaks very clearly to Zechariah and Elizabeth about the miraculous birth of their son, John the Baptist.

Luke 1:26-38 - The Lord speaks very clearly to Mary about the miraculous birth of Jesus, the Messiah.

Matthew 1:18-25 - God's assurance to Joseph concerning the miraculous conception of Jesus by His Holy Spirit. "Go ahead and marry her."

Acts 8:26-40 - "Now an angel of the Lord said to Philip, "Go south to the road the desert road that goes down from Jerusalem to Gaza." So he started, and on his way, he met an Ethiopian eunuch. "

Acts 9:1-6 - "As he neared Damascus on his journey, suddenly a light from heaven flashed around him. He fell to the ground and heard a voice say to him, "Saul, Saul, why do you persecute me? Who are you, Lord?" Saul asked. "I am Jesus, whom you are persecuting," he replied. "Now get up and go into the city, and you will be told what you must do."

Acts 10:1-33 - ". . . He distinctly saw an angel of God, who came to him and said, "Cornelius.. ." 9 About noon the following day, Peter went up on the roof to pray. He became hungry and wanted something to eat, and while the meal was being prepared, he fell into a trance. He saw heaven opened and something like a large sheet being let down to earth by its four corners. . .

Acts 13:1-5 " . . . While they were worshiping the Lord and fasting, the Holy Spirit said, "Set apart for me Barnabas and Saul for the work to which I have called them . . ."

Acts 15:28 - "It seemed good to the Holy Spirit and to us not to burden you with anything beyond the following requirements . . ."

Acts 16:6-10 - "Paul and his companions traveled throughout the region of Phrygia and Galatia, having been kept by the Holy Spirit from preaching the word in the province of Asia. When they came to the border of Mysia, they tried to enter Bithynia, but the Spirit of Jesus would not allow them to. So they passed by Mysia and went down to Troas.9 During the night Paul had a vision of a man of Macedonia standing and begging him, "Come over to Macedonia and help us."10 After Paul had seen the vision, we got ready at once to leave for Macedonia, concluding that God had called us to preach the gospel to them.

Acts 20:3, 13, 16 - ". . . Because the Jews made a plot against him just as he was about to sail for Syria, he (Paul) decided to go back through Macedonia. 16 Paul had decided to sail past Ephesus to avoid spending time in the province of Asia, for he was in a hurry to reach Jerusalem, if possible, by the day of Pentecost."

2 Corinthians 2:1- "So I made up my mind that I would not make another painful visit to you."

Titus 3:12 - "As soon as I send Artemas or Tychicus to you, do your best to come to me at Nicopolis, because I have decided to winter there."

PRINCIPLES

1. There is no set pattern regarding how God leads his children.

2. Sometimes, He makes His will, his plan quite clear, especially when the matter is of crucial importance to the progress of His kingdom.

3. Other times, He seems to allow us the freedom to use the intelligence and common sense He has given us to make decisions. Even then His Providence may override our unilateral decisions to accomplish His purposes in our lives.

4. Either way, we must have a heart that seeks to please Him and find His way, His will for us.

5. From the Biblical perspective, *God's will* is a secondary consideration and must always be discussed in the context of one's relationship with the Father. Therefore, the first step in *finding God's will* is to begin *to take seriously your relationship with Him* daily.

6. Consequently, it is in knowing God and committing your life and your future to Him, that his will has a way of working itself out in your life. Through the eyes of our faith, the Father will lead us where he wants us to go to do what He wants us to do if we love Him and want to follow Him.

7. God is ultimately more interested in your being His person, having a relationship with you, than in your doing something for Him.

QUESTIONS FOR REFLECTION

1. Up to this point in your life, what has been your modus operandi concerning big decisions in your life? Choose the best option below:

   a. I, more or less, have made my decisions with little or no regard for finding out *God's will*.

   b. I did my best to seek *God's will* through prayer and the counsel of others.

   c. I went ahead and made decisions, but had very little confirmation from God regarding whether or not they were *right or wrong* for my life.

   d. Quite, honestly I have never really struggled with this issue before.

2. True or False - *God's will* means that God has a detailed blueprint/plan for every person's life which He must reveal in whole or in part for them to fulfill his purpose for their lives.

3. What has been your most recent, satisfying experience of seeking/ finding God's leadership?

4. What about your most frustrating experience?

5. If your relationship with the Lord is the critical factor in all this, how is it going between you and Him at this point?

6. What circumstance in your life right now requires having a sense of God's leadership, and direction?

How God Reveals His Will

Through His written Word – the Bible – Psalm 119:105

Through the internal witness of His Spirit – John 14:16,17   16:13-15

Through the wisdom of others – Proverbs 15:22

Through circumstances – I Corinthians 16:8,9

Through your mind, common sense – Proverbs 16:9

Promises from God's Word about His Leadership, His Providence, and His Good Intentions for our lives (consider memorizing these verses)

Psalm 16:11   37:4,5   84:11 119:105

Proverbs 3:5,6   16:9   19:21

Isaiah 58:11

Luke 11:9,10

James 1:2-5

For Reflection & Prayer

Could you give specific examples from your life when the Good Lord has provided leadership in your life by each of the five means presented in the first section?

VIII. SUGGESTED READING
ANNOTATED BIBLIOGRAPHY

1. Bill Wallace of China – Jesse C. Fletcher (1931 -)
   When I was a Senior at Texas A&M, my pastor, Lloyd Elder, arranged a dinner meeting with Dr. Fletcher for me and several friends. As a result of that personal encounter, I read his biography of Bill Wallace, a Baptist missionary to China, who ends up a martyr for his faith - a very inspiring book at that point in my life.

2. Celebration of Discipline – Richard Foster (1942-)
   Foster makes a strong case for discipline as the key to a successful and fruitful Christian life. In the book, he deals with twelve classic disciplines – meditation, prayer, fasting, study, simplicity, solitude, submission, service, confession, worship, guidance, and celebration. His approach is both biblical and historical. He may stretch your idea as to what the Christian life is all about.

3. The Christian's Secret of a Happy Life - Hannah Whitall Smith, 1832-1911.
   Hannah Whitall Smith was an early Quaker. It is a delightful and insightful book that has stood the test of time, as it was first published in 1875 and is still available.
   This book was given to me in June of 1966 in Las Vegas, Nevada, by Mrs. Laurie Normandeaux. I was serving as a Baptist Student Union Summer Missionary and staying with her family for one week. We talked in the evenings about our lives in Christ and during one of those evening talks she told me that I had already met the girl I would marry in two years! As it happened, Melva and I met on June 6, 1966, and married on June 8, 1968.

4. The Company of the Committed – Elton Trueblood (1900-1994)
   Both of the books by Elton Trueblood were written during the *Church Renewal Movement* of the 1960s and 1970s. I encountered them as a college and seminary student as well as during my early years as a campus minister. The book titles give you a clue regarding the main focus of each book.

5. The Incendiary Fellowship – Elton Trueblood (1900-1994)
    See the above comments.

6. The Journal of George Fox – George Fox (1624-1691)
    He was an English Dissenter, opposing the Church of England, who
    was the founder of the *Religious Society of Friends*, commonly known
    as the *Quakers* or *Friends*. The son of a weaver, he lived in times of
    social upheaval and war. (Wikipedia) He was a prolific writer. The
    edition of his journal that I have is 600 pages!

7. The Journal of John Wesley – John Wesley (1703-1781)
    He was the Founder of the Methodist Movement in England. He was
    described by a contemporary as *"small in Stature; barely five feet six
    inches and weighing only one hundred twenty-two pounds, yet he was
    muscular and strong. Bright hazel eyes, fine features . . . "* Alexander
    Knox said of him, *"So fine an old man I never saw! The happiness of
    his mind beamed forth in his countenance. Every look showed how
    fully he enjoyed 'the gay remembrance of a life well spent.'"* [38] A
    fascinating book.

8. The Journal of John Woolman – John Woolman (1720-1772)
    He was a Quaker tailor in colonial New Jersey. His journal is a classic
    expression of the Quaker spirit at its best. It is a fascinating read both
    historically and spiritually. He was one of the very early opponents of
    slavery.

9. Keeping Your Eyes Open – William Roger Matkin (1945-)
    My first published book. It is a compilation of stories, metaphors,
    insights, and personal experiences, not organized around a particular
    theme. Often the inspiration came straight from the humdrum of
    daily living and the various arenas that defined my life as a husband,
    father, campus minister, carpenter, fisherman, hunter, and gardener.

---

[38] The Journal of John Wesley. Moody Press, Chicago, 1974, p. 25.

10. Lessons from Dr. Luke – William Roger Matkin (1945 -)
    For thirty-three years, from 1977-2010, we hosted medical and dental students and their spouses in our home for supper and Bible study. Because the author of the New Testament book of Luke was a medical doctor, I often chose it for our weekly studies, eventually covering the entire book. This book is a verse-by-verse study that includes commentary and suggested questions for reflection, and in a small group setting, for discussion.

11. Listening to Your Life – Frederick Buechner (1926-2022)
    The book is comprised of 366 thought-provoking and spiritually enriching daily meditations culled from Buechner's celebrated writings. He was a novelist, essayist, and preacher. Highly recommended.

12. The Spiritual Life – Evelyn Underhill (1875-1941)
    She was an Anglican mystic and theologian. As an evangelical Christian, read this little book with an open mind and you will be surprised and blessed. I found this book in the bookstore at Laity Lodge in June of 1986 as part of my research for my Doctor of Ministry Dissertation. It was recommended to me by Dr. Howard Hovde, Director of Laity Lodge at the time.

13. Through Gates of Splendor – Elizabeth Elliott (1926-2015)
    She was a Christian author and speaker. Her first husband, Jim Elliott, was killed, along with other American missionaries, while attempting to make contact with the Auca people of eastern Ecuador. Elizabeth later spent two years as a missionary to the tribe members who killed her husband. This book tells the exciting and tragic story of these five martyrs who paved the way for a breakthrough in taking the Gospel to the Auca people.

14. Tracks of a Fellow Struggler – John Claypool (1930-2005)
    John Claypool had the unique distinction of being both a Baptist minister and an Episcopal priest. My wife and I were members at Broadway Baptist Church in Ft. Worth when John was pastor. He was a masterful preacher and his sermons are available on the Internet.

This book was written in the aftermath of losing his twelve-year-old daughter, Laura Lue, to leukemia. He deals with the struggle of handling grief openly and honestly. He has written extensively and you would do well to seek out some of John's other books and listen to his sermons online.

Note: To my knowledge, the above books can be purchased online at Amazon Books either used or, in some cases, new printings. Many are classics, especially the journals, going back to the 1700s.

BIBLIOGRAPHY

Barclay, William. Daily Bible Study Series: The Letters to the Romans. Philadelphia: Westminster Press, 1955.

Beare, Francis W.. Interpreter's Bible, 11:188. New York: Abingdon, 1952.

Buttrick, G.A., Editor. Interpreter's Dictionary of the Bible. 4 vols. New York: Abington Press, 1962, 1:844.

Carson, Herbert M. Tyndale New Testament Commentary: The Epistle of Paul to the Colossians. Grand Rapids, Mich.:Eerdmans,1960.

Green, Michael. Tyndale New Testament Commentaries: The Second Epistle General of Peter. Grand Rapids, Mich: Eerdmans, 1968.

The Journal of John Wesley. Moody Press, Chicago, 1974.

Kelsey, Morton T. Companions On The Inner Way. New York: Crossroad, 1984.

McDowell, Edward A.. Broadmans Bible Commentary. 12:207. Nashville: Broadman Press, 1969.

Merriam-Webster Dictionary. New York: Simon & Schuster, 1984.

Miller, Keith. The Taste of New Wine. Waco: Word Books, 1965.

Morris, Leon. Tyndale New Testament Commentaries: The Gospel According to Luke. Grand Rapids, Mich.:Eerdmans, 1974.

Pringle, John, translator. Calvin's Commentaries. vol.11. Edinburgh: Calvin Translation Society, 1954.

Quoist, Michel. Prayers. Kansas City: Sheed and Ward, 1963.

Reid, James. Interpreter's Bible. 10:313,314. New York: Abington Press. 1952.

Simons, George F. Keeping Your Personal Journal. New York: Paulist Press, 1978.

Smith, Hannah Whitall. The Christian's Secret of a Happy Life. New Jersey: Revell Company, 1870.

Stott, J.R.W. <u>Tyndale New Testament Commentary: The Epistles of John</u>. Grand Rapids, Mich.: Eerdmans,1960.

Tasker, R.V.G. <u>Tyndale New Testament Commentaries: The Gospel According to Matthew</u>. Grand Rapids, Mich.: Eerdmans, 1961.

Thayer, Joseph Henry. <u>A Greek-English Lexicon of the New Testament</u>. New York: Harper and Brothers, 1889.

Tolbert, Malcolm O. <u>The Broadman Bible Commentary: Luke</u>, 12 vols. Nashville: Broadman Press, 1970.

Trueblood, Elton. <u>Alternative to Futility</u>. New York: Harper and Row), 1949.

Trueblood, Elton. <u>The Incendiary Fellowship</u>. New York: Harper and Row, 1967.

Vaughan, W. Curtis. <u>The Letter to the Ephesians</u>. (Nashville: Convention Press, 1963) Barclay, <u>William. Daily Bible Study Series: The Letters to the Galatians and Ephesians</u>. Philadelphia: Westminster, 1976.

Vine, W.E. <u>An Expository Dictionary of New Testament Words</u>. Nashville: Thomas Nelson, 1985.

Warren, Richard. <u>12 Dynamic Bible Study Methods</u>. S P Publications Inc., 1981.

<u>Webster's New World Dictionary</u>. New York: Simon & Schuster, 1982.

Wilder, Amos N. <u>Interpreters Bible</u> 12:254-255. New York: Abingdon , 1952.

Made in the USA
Monee, IL
18 April 2023

31849441R00095